BY LORI BORGMAN

My Memory is Shot; All I Retain Now is Water

The Death of Common Sense and Profiles of Those Who Knew Him

Catching Christmas

All Stressed Up and No Place To Go

Pass the Faith, Please

I Was a Better Mother Before I Had Kids

WHAT HAPPENS AT
Grandma's
STAYS AT GRANDMA'S

WHAT HAPPENS AT

Grandma's

STAYS AT GRANDMA'S

Lori Borgman

7747

WHAT HAPPENS AT GRANDMA'S
STAYS AT GRANDMA'S

Good Cheer Publishing

© 2019 by Lori Borgman
International Standard Book Number:
978-0-578-57021-1

Printed in the United States of America
Country Pines Printing
Shoals, Indiana

First Edition

For

The Grands

Love Always

Contents

Bonkers

I was confident I'd never go as bonkers as other women did when they became grandmothers. You know the ones — they see you at the grocery, whip out their cell phones, pin you against a wall of pasta and force you to look at picture after picture of their grandbabies. Meanwhile, your mocha fudge ice cream melts and the deli potato salad grows warm and sprouts botulism.

The truth is, I'm not really a small baby person. Preverbal creatures that communicate by crying have always put me on edge. When I was expecting, the books said not to worry because, as the mother, I would be able to distinguish one cry from another. The books lied. To this day when a newborn wails, I feel perplexed.

Stop crying and just tell me what you want. Talk to me. Move your lips. Anything. I'll figure it out. Just try! Diaper? You want a new diaper? I'll get you a new diaper. No? It wasn't the diaper? Please talk. I know you can't talk, but listen, I can get you a crayon and you can draw a picture of what you want. I'll even let you draw on the wall, just help me. No? What then? You're hungry? Great! We'll feed you. So, that wasn't it either. You weren't hungry? Then what? Please talk to me. Try talking to me with your eyes. Blink once for yes and twice for no. I think I'm getting something. Four legs and a tail? Neigh! You want a pony? Fine! I'll get you a pony!

Due to my limited abilities as a baby whisperer, I figured I'd be one cool cucumber when the grandbaby arrived. After all, it's not like we were becoming parents. We would take a backseat now. We would be second string, the B team.

Then it happened. Our son called midmorning and matter of factly said they were going to the hospital. A few text updates straggled in during the afternoon saying progress was slow. We packed our bags, preparing to leave the next morning. Finally, at 11:30 P.M. the call came, the wait was over. It was a baby girl. Momma and baby were both fine.

We fell into bed exhausted. Vicarious long-distance labor and delivery had been a lot more tiring than we had anticipated. The next morning, we hopped in the car and sped to Chicago to meet our first grandbaby.

I noted what good time we had made as the new grandpa left skid marks wheeling into a parking spot at the hospital. We hurriedly got directions at the front desk, sprinted down a hallway, caught an elevator to the third floor, dashed down another hallway, took a deep breath and slowly opened the door.

Our son stood leaning against a windowsill, holding a newborn swaddled in a soft white blanket with pink and blue stripes. The tiny bundle was topped with a white stocking cap. The delicate profile of a newborn protruded above soft folds in the blanket.

Our son was a father. The completely obvious was completely stunning.

Our daughter-in-law was radiant. She emitted the glow of motherhood. It agreed with her. It agreed with our son, too, but his was the glow of fatherhood. Or maybe it was a light sweat from anxiety.

They were both totally over the moon, enthralled and enraptured with their beautiful newborn. Bits and pieces slowly floated back to me. We had been over the moon, too. The marvel and wonder of new life takes your breath away.

The new momma and papa looked so young, so wide-eyed and dewy. What were they? Ten and twelve? Nah, they were in their midtwenties. Had we been that young?

We had. Even younger.

They were completely inexperienced.

So were we.

They seemed to be naturals — at ease with the baby, moving in tandem with a fluid motion.

Our son handed the baby to me. It was like cradling a bundle of feathers so light and soft. It's a different dimension when the baby you hold is your grandchild and not your own child. Because you're not the first line of defense, you relax more, take it all in more, savor it more, each flutter of the eyelids, each rise and fall of that tiny little chest.

When she cries, you won't be the one struggling to determine what she needs. It will be her parents' job to discover she wants a pony. As a grandparent, your job is to absorb it all, to be swept up in the wonder and marvel of a new life and the start of another generation.

The start of the next generation had mesmerized me with her delicate hands and button nose. This small being had smitten me. I was completely in her power. All I could think of was how I could never let this precious bundle go. Maybe I was going to be as bonkers as all the other grandmas. It would probably only be a matter of time before I pinned someone down in the grocery with pictures on my cell phone. Maybe I wouldn't even wait 'til the grocery. Maybe I'd pin someone down in the hospital on our way out.

She was so precious. So sweet.

I began thinking maybe I could take her home with us.

My daughter-in-law must have read my face, as she announced that the security tag on the baby's beautiful right leg would set off an alarm if somebody — anybody — tried to remove the baby from the premises.

I nodded and smiled at the daughter-in-law, who still glowed.

Then I whispered to the baby that Grandma could slip that security tag right off her little leg and we could give hospital security a run for their money.

I told her that Grandma had a vehicle ready to go in the parking lot.

I told her that Grandma would buy Peanut Butter Cap'n Crunch, hire circus clowns and let her stay up until midnight. I whispered in her little ear, asking if she wanted to come home with me.

The husband stepped up for his turn to hold the baby and read my face as well. He shot me a look and shook his head no.

I slowly returned to rational thought and reality. I took a seat in a chair, but my eyes never left the baby.

When we said our goodbyes, I looked at that precious bundle and her novice parents one more time. She opened her eyes. I held her gaze and communicated eyeball-to-eyeball and heart-to-heart. *They may look like they're rookies, but I think they know what they're doing. If you ever have any doubts, call me. Day or night. Grandma will always be here for you, Sweetie.*

She blinked. I think she understood.

Not So Fast, Baby

We were not so naïve when our first grandbaby arrived that we didn't realize we might be somewhat biased, although we sincerely did believe she was the most beautiful, brilliant, marvelous, delightful baby ever born.

When her weight and height fell to the 10th percentile on the growth chart, but her head remained in the 70th percentile, we said, "Fabulous! Wonderful! She needs a big head for that big brain. She's going to be an Albert Einstein or a Madame Curie!"

When the baby began scooting across the floor, tossing

aside plush toys, which were allergy-free and crafted for sensitive skin, in favor of the dog's toys — a matted stuffed opossum, tattered squirrel and mangy skunk — we said, "Astounding! The baby has a sixth sense for the animal world. The baby is going to be a Dr. Dolittle!"

When the baby attempted to put everything within reach into her mouth, including her own feet, the corners of rugs and her daddy's shoes, we said, "Amazing! Such a sense of curiosity. The baby is going to be an explorer and discover great things!"

When the baby rolled over to the dining room table and chairs and left bite marks on the chair legs, we said, "Look at that! The baby has a taste for woodworking!"

When the baby would no longer hold still for a diaper change, but would twist and squirm and weasel away, we said, "What agility! What form! The baby will be an Olympic gymnast one day! Or a great ballerina!"

When the baby could pull herself up by the stereo and rock out to "La Bamba" swaying back and forth, shaking her head, "singing" along, screaming "AEEEEEEEEEEEE" at a pitch that set dogs howling, we said, "Why, of course! The baby will be a musician! A composer! A choreographer!"

When the baby was at her Wiggle Worms class, crawled over to a little boy and planted a wet one on his check, plastering drool all over the side of his face, we said, "Astonishing! The baby has unbelievable interpersonal communication skills!"

When the baby sat up and turned her head whenever she heard the theme music on the Weather Channel, and did not tire of the punishing monotony, we simply looked at one another.

When the baby went to her other Grandpa and Grandma's house in the country where they have several dogs and the dogs lined up at feeding time and the baby crawled in line behind them, everyone was quiet.

When the baby had gathered a large admiring crowd of grandparents, aunts and uncles, and friends of the family and shoved her little finger up her little nose, no one said a thing.

When the baby did it again and again, deviating from the routine only to stick her little finger in her little ear, the crowd was mum.

"Oh my," someone finally said, breaking the silence.

"Goodness," muttered another.

"The baby is going to be a, um, a, the baby is going to be a — "BABY!" everyone shouted.

Have Gear, Will Travel

As newly minted grandparents who had been out of the baby business for a number of years, we had forgotten about the lopsided ratio between the size of a baby and the amount of gear a baby needs for travel.

When the grandbaby came for a visit, the trunk and backseat of their family car was crammed with baby paraphernalia. A neighbor asked if they were coming for the weekend or moving in.

All the baby-related gear must have weighed roughly 300 pounds and that figure did not include the baby's mother or father, the most essential travel gear of all. It was a 30:1 ratio, with 30 pounds of travel gear for every pound of baby.

It took five trips to lug it all into the house. When they were ready to leave two days later, it took 20 trips to get it all out. For a moment, it looked like they might have to rent a U-Haul. The fact that the baby stuff mushroomed is in no way the new parents' fault. Baby gear is like pasta salad and clothes hangers, it multiplies in the dark.

When a friend that our son used to go camping with stopped by to see the baby, I heard the new papa say, "Come on out to the car and see what we travel with — it's way more than we ever took camping." These guys used to fill the back of a truck with sleeping bags, tents, boots, waders, oars, rubber rafts and portable cookstoves.

Amateurs.

This baby could stuff all their camping gear in the cargo hold of her collapsible stroller and still have room for a pack of diapers and box of wipes.

It seems I had forgotten a number of things about newborns. Not only had I forgotten that no baby travels light, I also had forgotten it is easier to get a miniature Spandex swimsuit on a plastic Barbie with a 72-inch bust than to get a sleeper on an infant.

What's more, I'd forgotten that when babies gain control of their necks, they don't make smooth movements from side to side. They jerk their little heads with amazing force and speed. Babies are the original headbutters.

I'd also forgotten how babies can command an audience. One wail and every adult in the room is immediately on full alert.

I was also reminded that babies and their parents are primarily engaged in the business of waste management. Babies produce it and parents manage it. It may be the only industry that can consistently boast a satin-smooth bottom line.

What's more, I was reminded that babyhood is the only time of life in which people cheer you on for nonstop eating and sleeping.

When was the last time a family member exclaimed, "You took a two-hour nap in the middle of the day? Wonderful!"

When did your doctor ever say, "What you need to do is focus on consuming high-density calories and trying to pack some more fat on those thighs!"

For babies, it is a productive day if they eat, sleep, burp, and continually repeat the cycle.

It's good work if you can get it.

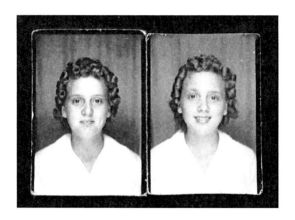

The Twists and Turns of Twins

My mother came from a brood of seven, which included younger sisters, Jean and Joyce, who were identical twins. She once used them for a 4-H project. She demonstrated a shampoo and set on one and the comb out on the other.

A picture of the twins with their home perms, which was taken in a dime store photo booth, shows them both smiling with a twinkle in their eyes that says they will get even with their older sister later.

Later came when they were in high school. Mom and the twins entered as a trio in a music contest. When it came time to perform, the twins refused to sing.

Perhaps the twins suddenly had laryngitis, or it was their way of telling Mom to go solo.

Aunt Jean and Aunt Joyce carried a touch of ornery. I never knew if they were born ornery or being twins made them ornery, but they were two of the most fun aunts any kid could ever have.

It is impossible to imagine one without the other because they were always "The Twins!" *(To be said with excitement as though a party is about to enter the room.)*

Because Jean and Joyce shared a powerful bond, when they married and began having children, both the twins named one of their daughters after the other twin.

Aunt Jean named a daughter Joyce, and Aunt Joyce named a daughter Jean. So, Aunt Jean and Aunt Joyce are sisters and Jean has a Joyce and Joyce has a Jean.

When Aunt Joyce had some health problems later in life, her daughter, Jean, was too overwhelmed to send out email updates, so Joyce, the daughter of Aunt Jean and niece of Aunt Joyce, sent out emails about Joyce and about taking her mother, Jean, to see Joyce and her daughter Jean.

In her emails, Joyce, the daughter of Jean, referred to Aunt Joyce, the sister of Jean, as Auntie J. Technically, Auntie J could be Aunt Jean or Aunt Joyce, so you really had to stop and think, was it Aunt Jean or Aunt Joyce who was ill, and was it Aunt Joyce or Aunt Jean who was well?

One day, when I spoke on the phone with Aunt Jean, the one who had been well, I broke the news to her that our daughter and son-in-law were expecting twins. "Identical twin girls!" I chirped.

Aunt Jean's response was immediate: "OH, NO!" she cried.

I had the impression Jean was speaking for Joyce as well, although I had yet to receive an email from Joyce, daughter of Jean, saying she had talked to Jean, daughter of

Joyce, and confirmed that Aunt Joyce shared the sentiment of Aunt Jean.

As of now, the twins-to-be have been going by the names on their ultrasounds — Baby A and Baby B. So far, so good.

Now if Baby A should grow up and have babies and name an offspring Baby B, and Baby B should grow up and have babies and name an offspring after Baby A, it will be an entirely different matter.

Preemies

Our family has been given many blessings, but height has never been one of them. So, we were surprised when our twin granddaughters arrived early and were being called the Big Kids on the Block. When you're closing in on 4 pounds in the neonatal intensive care unit, you qualify as middle linebackers.

Because the bruisers in soft pink and white sleepers were doing well and breathing on their own, they were promoted to the unit known as The Village. Technically, this made them Village People, although they were not able to jump up and sing "YMCA" with the accompanying arm movements. Maybe next week.

The two babies shared an Isolette, a large clear plastic box with an opening on each side and one on the end so caretakers can tend to the babies without changing their air temperature. Moms and dads were encouraged to do all the hands-on care in The Village, changing diapers, comforting the babies and taking the babies' temps at regular intervals.

The babies were swaddled separately amidst a tangle of wires for IV ports, heart, respiratory and oxygen monitors. There was a 10:1 blanket-to-baby ratio. Periodically, the Isolette looked like the morning after a slumber party. Blankets and bedding piled high in a wild disarray that said we stayed up all night, laughing, talking, drinking breast milk and having a ball.

The babies were mirror images of one another, perfect in every detail, from their little round heads, to their almond shaped eyes, tiny noses and rosebud lips. And yet, like all preemies, they were not quite finished. They were on the scrawny side for linebackers. Their little legs lacked meat and they would not be comfortable sitting on metal folding chairs.

There are three things preemies must learn to do when they are born. They must learn to breathe, feed and maintain their own body temperature. This is what was happening in the Isolette. One twin was doing this a little faster than the other.

But there was something else happening. The babies were freshly swaddled and positioned side-by-side. A space of 4 inches separated their little heads. One twin yawned, turned her head and the space between them narrowed ever so slightly. Then the other one stretched her neck and the space narrowed a little more. Slowly, almost imperceptibly, like a cloud gradually inching across a vast blue summer sky, the babies inched and wiggled until there was but a sliver of space between them.

In an effort to help the twin who was not quite as skilled at maintaining body temperature as the other one, a nurse swaddled them together in one blanket. Ah, heaven. They were now as close as they could be, not even a pinkie apart. The Isolette was covered with a heavy blanket enveloping the babies in shadows, simulating the environment in the womb.

A peek inside several minutes later revealed the baby who was maintaining temperature well had placed her small pink hand on her sister, who was struggling to maintain temperature, as if to say, "Don't worry, I'll warm you."

A few minutes after that, they were holding hands.

Two preemies in an Isolette already had what nearly all mankind longs for — someone to share the journey with, someone who will give you a pat on the head and someone to hold your hand.

ROCKING WALTER MATTHAU
TO SLEEP

There is an unwritten law that requires everyone to say that a baby is beautiful no matter what the baby looks like. You don't say that with preemies. You can, but people will know you are lying.

Preemies are a work in progress. Truthfully, they often look like baby birds. With preemies, you say, "They'll grow, they'll grow."

Then they do grow a little and they start looking like little old men. It's like rocking a miniature Walter Matthau to sleep in your arms.

Grandma Looks Like She Got Run Over by a Reindeer

Dark circles and bags under the eyes of mothers and fathers of newborns are badges of honor in parenthood. Those same dark circles and bags under the eyes of a grandma look like a woman with a drinking problem, aging before her time.

Sleep deprivation is never pretty. Consider the grandma, helping to care for newborn twins, who thought she accidently put a baby's sleeper in the Diaper Genie instead of the soiled diaper. The truly pathetic part is that the grandma shoved her hand into the Diaper Genie to check for the sleeper when she could have simply looked in the laundry basket for a soiled diaper.

The next night, Grandma changed both babies at 3 A.M. and three hours later was summoned to the nursery by the new mother, who was giggling. Both babies' diapers were riding several miles south of their plumbing systems. To my credit, the diapers would have caught any fluids that leaked from the babies' knees.

"Tsk, tsk," I say to my daughter as we study the low-slung diapers. "Who would have thought your precious preemies would be dressing like thugs?"

The babies, who still side with their new mommy and daddy on everything because their brains are not yet developed enough to know that grandparents are their true allies, begin thrusting their arms into the air as though they have questions.

You don't have to be a baby whisperer to know what they are asking.

"Is Grandma sober?"

Yes, Grandma is sober, Grandma is just very tired.

"If Grandma is sober, why does she bump into the walls at night and stagger when she walks?"

Because Grandma is not used to sleeping in 90-minute increments.

"Will we ever grow hair?"

"Who knows?"

"What is the square root of 81?"

"Nine. Now go to sleep."

Sleep deprivation is par for the course with newborns. When a clock says 12, you ask yourself if that is midnight or noon. It is no longer a concern that you put your contact lens in the wrong eye and wonder if that is Tartar Control Crest or Handers Buttocks Ointment you just squeezed on your toothbrush.

I am grateful for our youngest daughter who calls once a day and shouts into the phone, "TODAY IS WEDNES-DAY!" then hangs up. In desperate times, little things mean a lot.

Sometimes during the day, the new mommy and I encourage one another with exchanges like the following:

"You look like someone blacked both your eyes."

"Thank you. Your hair looks like it was caught in the blender."

"I know. You look like you were marooned on a desert isle."

And on it goes, until one of the babies shoots an arm into the air with another question.

"Yes, dear?"

"What time does the party start tonight?"

The babies know good and well when the party starts — the minute the heads of all adults in the house hit the pillows and they think they have a shot at sleep.

SMALL CHANGE

For weeks, life with the twins revolves around two charts on clipboards sitting on the kitchen counter. We must track all input and output to ensure the babies are making progress. We note how many ounces each drank from miniature-sized bottles. We note if a diaper was wet or dry. We note if the baby made a deposit in the diaper and the size of the deposit. A good deposit is the size of a quarter.

When I am back home, one time zone, three states and hundreds and hundreds of miles away, I will find myself gazing at quarters, treasuring memories of sleepless nights, endless crying and the bloom of love.

Babies on the Prowl

Rule No. 1 for living with babies: The greater the danger, the greater the force that pulls babies in that direction.

You think you covered all the electrical outlets and he finds the one outlet you overlooked. He had to wedge himself between the wall in the front entry and the legs of an antique hall tree made of oak, but he found it.

You blocked a pathway to danger behind the sofa by standing an ottoman on its side, jamming it between the back of the sofa and the French doors, and yet the floor lamp is now swaying. Funny, the floor lamp never swayed before.

He lifted the upholstered skirt on the ottoman, crawled through, lifted the skirt on the other side and found a new play area filled with office supplies, reams of paper, computer software, a floor lamp, books, books and more books.

Oh look, he is reading a 600-page volume on American history. Yes, really sinking his teeth into it. Page 232 to be exact.

Yesterday he had Dunkin' Donuts for breakfast. Ate half a coupon. He ate the donut half and was nutritionally astute enough to leave the part for the free coffee for a grown-up.

We stay ahead of danger by anchoring heavy objects, bolting doors and keeping shoes out of reach so they cannot be used as teething biscuits. We never suddenly back up in the kitchen without making three short high-pitched beeps like a heavy-construction backhoe. We keep constant vigil on the mass of cords beneath the computer desk. May you rest easy knowing that a baby can disrupt WiFi with a quick yank but cannot pierce an Ethernet cord with only two teeth.

Each morning he wakes up with one goal in mind — to perform death-defying acts that will prematurely age the adults in charge. He climbs up on the raised hearth in front of the fireplace and poses like an innocent cherub waiting for a camera. Don't be fooled — it's a ploy.

He grabs the handles on the fireplace doors, attempts to gain a toehold and scale the fireplace. In a split second, he pirouettes and lunges for the fireplace tools. Have you ever tried getting the upper hand on a 1-year-old waving a fireplace poker? Speak slowly, calmly and don't make any sudden moves.

If there is water within reach, babies will splash it.

If there is anything remotely hot in the vicinity, they will reach for it.

If it is shiny, they will smudge it.

If it is dirty, they will lick it.

If it is sharp, they will want it.

If it has a tag, they will chew it.

The sensible thing to do when babies are under your roof would be to build a padded cell. But what fun would that be and how would grandparents get any exercise?

SWEATING

I break out in a cold sweat whenever I change a diaper on one of these little ones. I worry I will break off an arm or a leg. Mothers don't forgive you for things like that. Not even your own daughter.

I carefully remove a teeny, tiny diaper and sweat. I tenderly lift two bony legs to clean a tiny, bony bum and sweat. I place a fresh miniature diaper under the tiny, bony bum and sweat. I gently pull the diaper up in the middle, in on the sides, secure it and sweat. I oh so carefully thread tiny breakable arms and tiny breakable legs back into the sleeves and legs of the sleeper and sweat. They babies are so very small and desperately need more meat on their little bones. If only I could be a donor.

This Baby is Berry, Berry Special

For years you think you'll never be more than a grandma to your grown children's dogs, then one grandbaby arrives, another follows, and the proliferation begins.

Our youngest is having another baby, her second baby, our ninth grandbaby, and we are weirded out.

Not about the baby. We're thrilled and excited about the baby. Couldn't be happier.

It's our daughter having the baby who is the concern.

She has a pregnancy app that tracks the baby's growth.

Lovely, right? Of course. What could be more beautiful than knowing the size of the new life growing within?

Except it doesn't track the baby in inches, or centimeters, or ounces, or pounds. It tracks the baby in fruit. Yes. Fruit.

She keeps sending disconcerting emails: "This week our baby is the size of a Maine blueberry."

I love Maine and I love Maine blueberries. Hands down, they are the best blueberries for baking. I'll probably never eat another one.

The next week, I was sent a notification saying, "Baby is now the size of a wee raspberry." Raspberries are my second favorite fruit after blueberries. At least they used to be.

The week after that, the baby was the size of a southern pecan. It's one thing to mess with fruits, but pecans? That is flat out nuts.

I called her up and asked her to stop.

"Stop what?"

"Stop ruining food for me with the baby tracker emails. You're not growing a fruit salad, you're growing a baby, and in the meantime, the food trackers are making me nauseous."

"Not a problem," she said. "I can also chart the baby's growth with vegetables — Brussels sprout, bok choy, corn on the cob, cabbage and eggplant."

"You just ruined any remote possibility I ever had of going vegan."

"The app can also be set to track the baby in relation to desserts," she said. "I tried that, but one week it said Charlotte royale and I had no idea what that was."

"You are on dangerous mounds of meringue messing with desserts." I snapped.

"They also have animals. This week the baby is the size of a guinea pig, then next week a chinchilla, then a prairie dog."

"Stop. Just stop."

"Wait. There's one more option. I can track baby growth in objects" she says. "This week the baby is the size of a paper airplane. Next week it will be the size of a baseball cap, then a water bottle."

"You realize that makes no sense, right? How can a baby go from the size of a paper airplane to a baseball cap?"

"I think the cap is rolled up."

"Oh, I guess that does makes sense. Listen, you're ruining fruits, vegetables, small furry animals and ball caps, but before I block your emails, just out of curiosity, what fruit is week 40?"

"Watermelon."

I should have seen that one coming.

The Stork Has Landed

Not every baby takes nine months to arrive. Some take years.

Couples longing to be parents, and parents longing to be grandparents, wonder if a baby will ever arrive. The yearning is palpable. The ache is mostly silent but deep.

She's in her thirties now, the little girl who grew up two doors down the block. She became a phenomenal teacher that parents clamor for. While loving, nurturing and teaching other peoples' children, she longed for a child of her own.

She and her husband have had their nursery set up for two years. The white crib with the soft green blanket hanging over the side stands by the window. Wooden cutouts of smiling farm animals, a pig, a sheep, and a cow, hang on the wall. A needlepoint pillow that her mother stitched sits alone in the rocking chair.

The layette is complete with green and yellow sleepers, booties and little hats, every tiny article of clothing lovingly arranged in the dresser drawers. They are prepared for either a boy or girl.

Several expectant mothers have looked at the hopeful couple's "book" as they say in the adoption world. The "book" is where you tell about yourself, your life, your views, what you might offer a child in the way of family. You include spontaneous pictures of yourselves doing everyday things. Spontaneous pictures carefully posed. It's an uncomfortable way to convey information. It feels like marketing.

Every weekend she and her husband go shopping and buy one new thing for the baby they don't have — a car seat, a rattle, a stroller, a stuffed animal, more diapers.

A year drags by and they change adoption agencies. Several months later, they have a match. A birth mother wants them to have her baby. They count down the months, imagining innumerable scenarios for an on-time delivery, an early delivery and a late delivery.

The due date arrives and the birth mother delivers a healthy full-term baby. Then the birth mother changes her mind.

They are devastated. They grieve and mourn for the baby they were ready to love. They are awash in devastation and grief.

Her parents worry about her. About them both. How much more can they endure?

The young couple resumes a facsimile of the routine when one morning the phone rings. There is a baby. The mother has already delivered and she wants them.

Sorrow kisses you on one cheek; joy on the other.

Within hours they are packed and in the car. They arrive at their destination and tell the hotel clerk they don't know how long they'll be staying because they are in town to adopt a baby and it may be several days before the baby is released.

Grandparents are glued to their phones. Updates seem sparse and far apart.

When the young couple returns to their hotel room that night, they walk into their room and find a new baby blanket sitting on their bed. It is from the hotel manager and the desk clerk.

Maybe the hotel staff felt the excitement and the apprehension. Maybe they've walked a similar path in one direction or the other.

The baby is released to the young couple the next day and the new mother and father contemplate the drive home. They aren't about to take the interstate, where maniacs can fly by at 85 mph oblivious to the fact that a precious three-day-old baby will be snuggled in a car seat in the backseat of the car.

Then they do what a lot of new parents do. They worry. They worry about the baby. They worry about the heat. They worry about whether the car will break down. It never has, but it has never carried such fragile hopes and dreams before either.

They decide it will be safer and easier to pull off on small roads should a need arise, so they take the roads less traveled, state highways and back roads all the way home.

At long last, the crib has a little one to hold. The farm animals on the wall have someone to watch. The rocking chair has reason to rock. A new mother and father, and new grandparents, have reason to cry tears of joy.

Fit to be Tied

Whenever we transport a little one, our kids insist on putting the car seats in our vehicle for us. They don't trust us to do it.

Cars seats are complicated today. They are also a major investment, not just in a child's safety, but a financial investment. When our daughter-in-law told us the price of a car seat they were buying, I thought, "Well, the kid can kiss higher education goodbye."

The silver lining to this cloud is that the child can stay in the car seat until she actually goes to college, as it will hold a person who is 62 inches tall and weighs 120 pounds.

You don't simply buy a car seat today; you go for a fitting. Stores let prospective buyers take a car seat off the shelf and tote it to the parking lot to try it out in their vehicle. The experience is like test driving a car, but you never leave the lot and don't get to enjoy the new-car smell.

If you like the car seat, and it fits with the dimensions of other car seats for your other children, you return to the store and sign up for the 10-year payment plan. Just kidding. You swipe your plastic and wait for the pain that will come at the end of the next month.

Today's car seats feature steel frames, impact-absorbing bases, cushy upholstery, nine-position harnesses, orthopedic back support, tilt options and beverage cup holders.

Our children rode in molded infant car seats that were basically open buckets on an incline with a strap holding them in place. There wasn't the convenience of snapping a carrier in and out of a base. My generation of mothers lunged into back seats, wrenching our spines, twisting our necks and shoulders and throwing hips out of joint to secure a baby in a car seat. This is also why we stayed home a lot.

Our grown children, all married and parenting infants and toddlers of their own, have asked how our parents traveled with us in automobiles when we were infants. I tell them that our mothers and fathers just let us roll around on the floor of the backseat, because that's what their parents did. They thought it would build character.

Truthfully, I think we were toted about in little baskets that were placed on the front seat or the floor of the front passenger seat. For toddlers there were child safety seats, a contraption that hooked over the front passenger seat, the most dangerous seat in a vehicle.

When you were bigger, you could stand in the backseat and have a good view through the front windshield. You steadied yourself when the car was in motion by gripping the back of the driver's seat. It was a fine system until your dad had enough, gave your hands a swat with his meaty paw and said to sit down and quit pulling on his seat.

Naturally, the kids are horrified by all this. I gently explain that it was looser back in the day. It was so loose that some kids stretched out on the ledge below the back window. A snooze and a tan all at the same time.

Our adult children look at us like we are crazy and give each other knowing nods that imply, "That certainly explains a lot, doesn't it?"

That's when I tell them about seat belts. There weren't any. At least not until the late Sixties. The only seat belts were human. If you were riding in the front passenger seat and your mom or dad had to brake suddenly, they flung their right arm out and smacked you in the chest. They belted you and held you in the seat all at the same time — a seat belt.

My mom was a nervous driver and tended to slam on the brakes even when it wasn't necessary. Consequently, I frequently got the arm smack across the chest. Even after seat belts became standard in cars, she would still fling out her arm and smack us across the chest out of habit. A lot of teen girls, myself included, thought that is why we were flat chested for so long.

Of course, ages ago, we were also allowed to ride in the back of pickup trucks. That sounds so egregious in light of today's safety standards that I make a point of saying that the wind blowing in your face on a hot summer day, your hair whipping your face and watching dust clouds roll on a gravel road, was not fun. Not at all. Not in the least tiny bit. Riding in the back of a pickup today is something I'm not sure even dogs are allowed to do. Nor should they. Put them in a dog seat. At least until they are 62 inches or weigh 120 pounds.

SNIP, SNIP

"Mommy wants to trim the bushes, Grandpa. She said to tell you to bring the head trimmers when you come.

Naming Grandpa and Grandma

Expecting couples often ask the soon-to-be grandparents what they would like to be called when the baby arrives. This task is often presented to grandparents as a means of keeping them occupied and, hence, too distracted to offer a lot of unsolicited advice.

We knew that Oma and Opa, would not be contenders. Oma was my mother-in-law's given name and it will always belong to her. Besides that, the companion to Oma is Opa. Although Opa is German for Grandpa, it always reminds me "My Big Fat Greek Wedding." I hear Opa and look around assuming that toasting and dancing is about to commence.

Nana and Papa were possibilities, but Nana had already been cornered by several close friends. Besides, in my mind, Nana conjures up a woman whose hair is always in place and coordinates her shoes and purse. That's not me.

A friend knew that she wanted her mother and father to go by Mamaw and Papaw long before any grandbabies were on the scene.

I considered I might be a grandma by association, like both of my grandmothers had been. My maternal grandmother, the hardworking farm wife with sturdy arms, a hug and big smile when you walked in the door, the one who sometimes let us gather eggs with her in the hen house, was Grandma Larry.

My paternal grandma, the one who could have her

pocketbook on her arm and be ready to go on a moment's notice, the one who could play any song in any key on a piano or church organ, was Grandma Judy. Both grandmas had tagalong babies when they were approaching 50. Those tagalongs were still living at home when we came on the scene. We called them both Grandma in person, but their destination names were Grandma Larry and Grandma Judy, both grandmas identified by the last child living at home.

I love children, but it was a giant exhale when I passed 50 and did not find myself taking a home pregnancy test or shopping for maternity clothes.

When our first grandchild came along, it looked like we might be Abuelo and Abuela. Our daughter-in-law, a foreign language teacher, was teaching their little one Spanish. The husband quickly evolved into Abuelo Cheese because he takes a lot of pictures and is always telling people, "Say cheese!"

I eventually became Abuela Beep-Beep because I sometimes cooked dinner when we went to visit and often managed to set off the smoke detector. Beep! Beep! Beep! Beep! Hence Abuela Beep-Beep. My cooking skills are legendary — in a fire extinguisher sort of way.

The ones that still call us Abuelo and Abuela from time to time call their other set of grandparents Grandma and Grandpa Whitey. It is another example of grandparent by association. Whitey is a dog.

Most often we are referred to as Grandma and Bobby. It always amuses me to hear, "Grandma and Bobby are here!" or have a kid charge into the house, yelling, "Where's Bobby?"

It sounds like we divorced, and I remarried some guy who came on the scene late in the game. It is fun to be out and about, run into someone we know and see the looks on their faces when one of the grands calls the husband Bobby. Who's Bobby? Is the man they know leading some sort of double life? Maybe they don't know him as well as they thought.

The husband became Bobby because the "buh" sound is one of the first sounds babies can make. Buh-buh-buh-bobby.

When they're not using our Spanish monikers, or Grandma and Bobby, we're just plain old Grandma and Grandpa, and that suits us fine, too.

Heeeere's Bobby!

For years now, experts have been saying that people should plan on having more than one career in a lifetime. Good thing I listened to the experts, otherwise I might have been caught off guard to find myself suddenly married to a rock star.

The husband didn't start out as a rock star. He has been a news photographer and journalist all his working years.

He didn't become a rock star until he became a grandpa.

These days, fans yell and scream and jump out from behind doorways, bushes and furniture whenever they spot him. They run at him, charge at him, hang on his legs, jump on his back and nearly knock him down. If ever a man needed a security detail, it is this one.

To be clear, the husband doesn't have millions of fans — more like a dozen. What his fans lack in number, they more than make up for in volume . . .

"Bobby!"

Scream it like his fans do!

They don't follow his every move on Facebook or Twitter, but they do follow him through the house, the backyard and a nearby park.

How does one shoot to rock star sensation level overnight? You become a human jungle gym. You let one kid ride on your back and carry two more, one in each arm. You give horsey rides to two and three fans at a time. You let fans play with your reading glasses, twist the arms, bend the frames and even use them for hide and seek. You begin buying cheap glasses in packs of three at the Dollar Store so as not to disappoint your fans.

You let your fans sit in your lap when they eat dinner (to their parents' chagrin). You let them play with the comb in your back pocket (and lose it). You let them take pictures on your smart phone (bursts, dozens at a time).

You become an overnight rock star by sheer charm and

personality. You hold mini pretzels in front of your eyes like they are glasses. You achieve hero status diving into the thicket to retrieve the ball. You courageously declare that anytime is a good time for ice cream.

You become a rock star by drawing funny pictures and reading books. Book after book, sometimes the same book after book — books about crocodiles, birds, bears, mice, machinery and talking vegetables.

Being married to a rock star has its challenges. Some days the fans pass me right by as they sprint to the main attraction. It's OK. Somebody has to stay grounded. Somebody has to be responsible, pay attention to safety, nutrition and assess what bones might break if a small fan were to fall from a particular height.

The fans are gone now. The rock star is recovering on the couch in a deep sleep. He'll probably want dinner when he regains consciousness.

Mine may not be a glamorous job, but somebody has to manage the talent.

He's Glad You Asked

The husband refuses to listen when I tell him that he shouldn't carry on so about our grandkids to other people who have grandkids as well. "They think their grandchildren are just as special as ours," I say.

He staggers backward. His jaw drops and the color drains from his face. He is stunned. Clearly, the thought has never crossed his mind that there might be grandchildren equally spectacular, or even more spectacular (as if that's possible!) than ours.

The husband's problem, and this has always been his problem since the day I met him, is that he is sincere and kind. Being a sincere and kind individual, when someone asks about the family, he truly thinks they mean it. He thinks they want details. Oh, he'll give you details all right. Age, height and weight percentiles, who is potty trained, who is walking, who knows their ABCs and which ones prefer the sandbox over the kiddie pool.

If you're still standing and your eyes are still open when he takes a breath, he will mistake this as genuine interest. He will then continue, telling you which ones appear to have an aptitude for engineering, which ones seem drawn to the arts and which ones he thinks may one day win Pulitzers.

The husband once chased a man out of a wedding reception yelling, "Wait! I wasn't finished! What's your email? Want me to text you? Don't worry! I'll find you on LinkedIn! What was your name again?"

I'd never seen a set of taillights speed away so fast.

Not that the man brags, but the man brags — without shame and without apology.

To be honest, he thinks there may be something wrong with grandparents who do not brag about their grandchildren. Come to think of it, he could be right.

What kind of person wouldn't want to tell stories about listening to his grandbaby giggle into the phone? What kind of person wouldn't show a hundred of his closest friends the silly dances his grandchildren created?

Still, the husband may be in a league of his own. For him, grandkids are better than a Beatles reunion, ESPN, ESPN2 and the Cincinnati Reds winning the World Series. Yep, grandchildren top all those things and that's why he loves to talk about them.

That said, if you run into us, don't ask about the family.

If you do ask about the family, try not to give him verbal encouragement.

If you do give verbal encouragement, and he offers to show you pictures and dives for his cell phone, I have one word of advice — run!

Grandma Guilt

For nearly three years, I've been waiting for this moment. Our oldest granddaughter has lost a tooth. It's not the first tooth she has lost, just the first tooth she has lost naturally.

She lost her first tooth when she was two. At our house. On the patio. She was running and fell face down. Blood everywhere. Blood and crying. Blood and crying are like the chicken and the egg. You don't know which comes first and it doesn't matter. They come together — profusely and loudly.

Should such a thing happen on your patio, let me save you time. Don't bother finding the tooth, submerging it in milk, or frantically searching for a dentist who will call you back on a Sunday afternoon. The tooth is history.

The toddler will live with a gap and you'll live with grandma guilt. That's right, just when you were shedding the last layers of mother guilt, you now don the heavy cloak of grandma guilt.

Every time the little one missing a front tooth smiled, I felt responsible. Sure, I didn't have anything to do with it and her parents and other adults were present, but it happened at our house. Grandma's house is supposed to be a fun and happy place, not a place where you go to get your teeth knocked out.

I was so sorry it happened and especially sorry that if something like this had to happen, that it couldn't have happened at her other grandma's house. But then her other grandma doesn't have a concrete patio. She does have a lot of gravel and steep hills though. Oh well, it happened here.

Our son and daughter-in-law got over it quickly. They never let it become an issue. The smile with the missing tooth gradually became part of who their little girl was. She'd smile and the missing front tooth said, "I have charm, personality, and do not mess with me on the playground." If others noticed the missing tooth, they didn't inquire.

(Thank you.)

Now she has lost her front bottom tooth, directly below the missing top tooth, which means one really great thing — she has a gap. A marvelous, wonderful gap. Do you know what fun a gap is? You can do great things with a gap.

She'll be the centerpiece of every Christmas celebration this year singing, "All I Want for Christmas is My Two Front Teeth."

She can insert straws in the gap, do tricks with her tongue in the gap, shoot water through the gap and, in general, perform dazzling feats that will make her the envy of every other child at the kids' table come holiday time.

She can whistle through that gap.

She can leave unique teeth tracks in a banana.

A gap puts her in the same category as famous actors, actresses and supermodels. Granted, their gaps align a different way and are substantially smaller, but still.

The best thing about having a gap is that it means your permanent teeth are coming soon and Grandma will let herself off the hook.

Air Mattress

There are many ways grandparents demonstrate love, but the greatest of all may be sleeping on an air mattress.

We have just returned from a visit with our son, daughter-in-law and five children who live in a three-bedroom apartment in Chicago. Their motto is "Stack 'em High and Stack 'em Deep."

The third bedroom is an overstatement. It is more like a generously sized pantry. It houses toys, blocks, games and a changing table for the baby.

It also houses us. It is where we sleep on an air mattress when we visit.

Our son and a couple of the kids inflate the air mattress on its side, then slowly, and oh so carefully press the air mattress down, wedging it between the changing table, a shelving unit and a wall.

Because an air mattress wedged on three sides is basically a bounce house, the kids jump on it and whoop and holler until someone yells, "Knock it off! That's Grandma and Grandpa's deluxe accommodations!"

The last time we were there, I crawled onto the air mattress at the end of an exhausting day and fell sound asleep. Several hours later, the husband came to bed, dropped his full weight onto his side of the air mattress and sent me flying. Shortly before midnight I went from being sound asleep to being wide awake, airborne and screaming.

We have slept on air mattresses in three states. Grandchildren have lived a three-hour drive away, a one-day drive away and a two-day drive away. As of this writing, we are blessed to have a half dozen of them less than a half hour away. We do not take this for granted. We have friends with grown children and grandchildren living overseas.

When we had our first baby, and our second, and our

third, we lived 2,000 miles from family. It felt like a dreadful distance. And yet.

And yet when family came, they didn't come for coffee, a rushed meal or tag us on to a list of errands. They came for days. Or weeks.

Extended stays meant you were there for bath time for little ones, bedtime rituals, tousled hair and morning cereal. Extended visits were relaxed and casual, a sightseeing trip or two, but also just sitting, talking, folding laundry, reading books to the children, coloring with them and playing games, taking walks, preparing meals and doing dishes.

There is a blend of closeness and chaos when family unpacks and you do life together under one roof. You come to know one another in different dimensions.

She cleans the kitchen floor almost every night after the kids are in bed.

Leave an unattended glass on the counter and he will whisk it into the dishwasher before you can say, "Where's my water?"

They have "quiet hour" before putting the kids down at night. The lights are turned low, they use soft voices and read books. "Quiet hour" is wonderful in theory, but is the loudest hour of the day.

They eat at home more than they eat out. Parks and trails are weekend favorites. They are genuinely kind to one another, thoughtful of one another.

The little ones like back rubs before they go to sleep.

The oldest tot is up before the sun.

When family lives away, you go places you might not

otherwise have gone. You see different shorelines, night skies, storm fronts and cityscapes you might not otherwise have seen. You may hear the wind howl as it tears through a small Oklahoma prairie town at night, or fall asleep to the rumble of elevated trains weaving through a bustling city.

When the visit is over, you pack your clothes and your memories, say your goodbyes, stifle your tears and head home. All the while, thinking and planning for next time, and dreaming of the day they might live closer.

Good Talkers

There is no greater delight as a grandparent than having your kids trust you with their kids and being willing to let them stay for an overnight or two. Or even a week and a half in exceptional cases. Naturally, you do everything in your power to ensure that the stay goes well and yields nothing but good reports so you might be trusted again one day.

If you overlook the 6-year-old demonstrating her best soccer kick, whereupon her shoe flew off her foot and grazed the side of my head, we had a good visit with two of the grands.

When our son and his wife had their fourth child we drove to Chicago, admired the new baby, then brought the

6- and the 4-year-old home with us for 10 days. Make that 10 days and six hours, but who's counting?

Occasionally, on long drives, I sometimes grow drowsy, but this was not a remote possibility with our inquisitive passengers in the car.

"Where does gasoline come from, Grandma?"

"What's the difference between a golfer and a gopher, Grandpa?"

I would have said the difference between a golfer and a gopher is an "l" and a "p," but their grandpa is more patient than their grandma.

"What exactly is quicksand?"

They had a steady barrage of questions that could have kept us googling for hours.

"What if hail comes down on your house?"

It was like a game show with only seconds to answer before another question was fired.

"How do the police catch bad guys?"

"You're good conversationalists," I told the kids. "Do you know what that means?"

"Yes, it means we're good talkers."

The good talkers came with, shall we say, an intensity.

"It's going well," I told a friend on day four. "Although it is a bit of a jolt to our systems."

Two days later I considered instituting nap time. For the adults.

We gravitate toward conversational tones; the children were propelled by sudden bursts of shrieking and laughing. I've always enjoyed the piano against the wall where it has stood for 20 years, but they moved it perpendicular to the wall to create a fort.

"How is it going?" our son asked by phone.

"They're angelic," I said. (When they are sleeping.)

"Are they behaving?" he asked.

"Oh my, yes." (Do not get out of that chair until I say you can!)

"Are they eating well?"

"Very well." (If you count cheese as a food group.)

I was making calzones one afternoon when my garlic disappeared. I entertained the idea that I had finally lost my mind. Still, I looked high and low, searching the kitchen and finally asked out loud how a woman loses six garlic bulbs in a mesh tube.

"Were they in that thing that looks like a sock?" one of them asked.

"Yes."

"I took it upstairs to play with it."

It was wonderful to have them here for a lengthy stay.

We called the day after we delivered them back home and asked how they had adjusted to one another again.

"It was sure quiet when they were gone," our son said.

"It's great to have them back. It's just a bit of a jolt."

We understand.

CLEAN SWEEP

"Grandma, do you mop?"
 "Sometimes. Why?"
"Here, and here, here and . . . "

Don't Anybody Touch My Stuff

We are all attached to stuff. Most of us like to think we are generous with the stuff we have, and to some degree or another we are, or least we give that appearance. But the truth is, there are some things we clutch tightly and have no intention of sharing.

I often wonder how the attachment to stuff takes root. Then one day I saw it take root right before my eyes, in small grandchildren who at times could pass for short adults without the polish and veneer.

The twins have recently turned 3 and are with their 1-year-old sister in the attic of the old New Jersey farmhouse where they live. The attic has small paned windows with thick wavy glass on either side of where a chimney once stood. The gabled ceiling cocoons the wide-open space, creating an idyllic place for play.

One of the twins announces she needs to use the potty, which is down the steep, narrow stairs and at the end of the hall on the floor below.

She pauses at the top of the stairs, tosses back her head of curls, and sweetly says, "Don't anybody touch my stuff."

She could have said, "Be right back," or "Will someone go with me?" but instead she fired a shot across the bow. Granted, it was a pink, fluffy shot covered in feathers, but it was a shot, nonetheless.

She pauses halfway down the steps and sweetly calls

out again, "Don't anybody touch my stuff!"

The door at the bottom of the stairs creaks as she opens it.

"Don't anybody touch my stuff!" she sings.

"Nobody is touching your stuff!" her mother calls back. "We don't even know what stuff is your stuff!"

Her stuff could be the small naked doll with the cloth body, the Elmo slippers or the purse in the shape of an alligator.

It could be the plastic Cozy Coupe that has already been sideswiped twice this morning and rolled once. Whatever her stuff is, we know this much — we are not to touch it.

She leaves the door to the attic open and we hear footsteps padding down the hall. The toilet lid goes up with a clunk. "Don't anybody touch my stuff!" she shouts.

This is a child who usually insists on privacy, but today she is deeply concerned about her stuff.

The toilet flushes.

"Nobody touch my stuff!"

The step stool scrapes across the floor as she pushes it to the sink. This is followed by the sound of running water.

"Nobody is touching your stuff," I yell. "Your stuff is plastic, and Grandma only likes plastic in the shape of small cards with magnetic stripes on the back."

In the child's defense, her younger sister has been dubbed "Swiper" for grabbing whatever is of interest to her twin sisters. When you live with someone nicknamed Swiper, perhaps you are never truly at peace that your stuff is safe.

She climbs up the stairs still sing-songing, "Don't anybody touch my stuff!"

As it turns out, the stuff she is concerned about is a doll stroller and a pair of pink plastic high heels. This is the equivalent of a convertible to a man in midlife crisis and a pair of Jimmy Choo's for a twentysomething female.

We are all a touch possessive about our stuff. We can even be annoying about our stuff. But at least as adults, we're too sophisticated to go around saying, "Don't anybody touch my stuff!"

The one concerned about others touching her stuff seats herself at the little table and begins coloring with her twin, who has been quietly taking it all in. Swiper is in another corner of the attic, momentarily entertaining herself.

In a sweet voice, barely above a whisper, the twin who has been at the table coloring looks at her sister and says, "The next time you leave, I'm gonna touch your stuff."

PETER RABBIT

Driving along and a rabbit crosses the road.
Driver: "I wonder if that is Peter Rabbit?"
Grandkid: "Does he have on a blue jacket?"

My Name is on the Bathroom Wall

It wasn't until I was a grandma that my name and phone number were plastered on a bathroom wall. My contact info, along with my picture, are on the bathroom wall where one of the grands is potty training.

When she has a success, she chooses someone to call and then that person emotes through the phone, shouts, yells, claps and cheers her on to greatness. Or dryness.

The husband just got a text saying that if he doesn't take his phone off mute and field a few calls he's going to be deleted from the call list. Just like that, Grandpa could be history. The world of potty training is brutal. But then, it always has been.

Potty training is right up there with your kid getting a driver's license — a milestone that you, the parent, simultaneously look forward to and dread.

When our daughter said she was using the "Potty Training in a Day" method, I didn't say anything.

A lot of people who speak with an air of authority say that grandmas aren't supposed to offer their opinions unless they're asked. So, I keep mine to myself. That was a joke. Although sometimes, I do try.

When our daughter said you give the child a doll that goes potty, I didn't say anything.

When she said you give the child salty snacks and drinks and have them practice running to the potty, I didn't say anything.

When she said you reward the kid with M&Ms, I finally

spoke up and said, "Somebody gave me a book just like that when your brother was born. I started the 'Potty Training in a Day' method on a Monday and threw it across the room on Thursday.

"I gained five pounds from rewarding myself with M&Ms every time your brother went potty. Thirty years later and I'm still trying to lose the weight."

Of course, these days there are endless options when it comes to potty training. There's "Potty Training Your Child in a Week," "Potty Training Your Child in Three Days" and "Potty Training Your Child in Less Than One Day." I would think the Less Than One Day method would be far more appealing than Potty Training in a Week. Who wants to drag it out if you don't have to?

To our daughter's credit, she was more diligent than I was, and her little girl was ready and caught on quickly. Also, to our daughter's credit, she didn't post any pictures of it on Facebook.

Despite the recent family success with "Potty Training in One Day," my favorite approach floating around right now is "The Naked & $75 Method," which comes from John Rosemond. You let the kid run around naked for three days, the theory being that the kid won't like the mess and will get to the potty on his or her own.

The $75 is for cleaning the carpet.

STRAIGHT FLUSH

"Gwama, the toiwet is broke."
(The handle had come off.)

"It comed off. I wonda what happnd."

"I wonder, too."

"Maybe Gwanpa bwoke it."

How Taft May Have Gotten Out of the Tub

I was recently asked if I was alive when Aesop wrote all those fables.

"Not quite, dear. He was a few years ahead of me."

Aesop lived sometime between 620 and 564 B.C. Few things age you more than realizing your grandchildren consider you may date all the way back to antiquity.

That said, history with Grandma is fun because Grandma is old enough she might have been there and, even if Grandma wasn't there, she tells the story like she was.

We are having lunch with several of the grands, eating on plastic place mats that feature the United States presidents on one side and the three branches of government on the other.

"Who is that one by Roosevelt?" one of the girls asks.

"That is Taft. He was the heaviest president in history. The man weighed more than 300 pounds," I state, as though I personally conducted the weigh-in.

Clearly, they are disturbed by the news. Attempting to ease their anxiety, I say, "He probably should have eaten more vegetables."

"I'd like to know more about Taft," one says wryly, insinuating that my claim about Taft's bulk warrants verification. She is the same one who still suspects I was a contemporary of Aesop.

"There is a story that he was so big, he got stuck in the

bathtub."

"Grandma!" they shout in unison, as though I am telling such a whopper that lightning may strike.

"It's true," I say.

"I'd like to see the tub," states the skeptic who will one day be a prosecuting attorney.

We look it up on the internet and see that it was a tub specially built to hold four men and, in fact, four fully-clothed men are pictured sitting in the tub posing for a photograph.

They are quiet, mulling over the dilemma.

"Did they have phones?" says the one, who is the unofficial event planner in the group.

"Honey, not even a smart phone could have helped the man get out."

"Why didn't he just hold onto the bathtub and jump?"

"He was wedged," I said. "The story is that they tried using butter — "

"That wouldn't work," interrupts the event planner. "Curious George got his leg stuck in a trash can and at first the Man in Yellow used butter, but it didn't work, so they had to call the fire people. They had to use a saw to cut George out. Maybe they sawed the bathtub, spread it and then he got out."

"Maybe," I say.

"Or, or, or — " Her brain is at full-throttle in problem-solving mode. "He must have filled the bathtub more because when you fill it with water — fill it up super high — he could go higher and take a breath and then pull up."

The skeptic in the group, frustrated by all the specula-tion and lack of concrete answers, jumps off her chair and exits the kitchen shouting, "I just wanted to know how he got out of the tub!"

The event planner, satisfied that either a fire depart-ment arrived and used Jaws of Life, or that Taft dislodged himself relying on the mechanics of displacement, gazes at the place mat then ruefully says, "My favorite president was Washington, but now it's this one — Tadd."

SINGING IN THE CAR

Four-year-old:
"Life is good. Life is good. Life is good.
Life is good. Oooooooooooh.
Life is good."

Naughty or Nice?

One of the best gifts we ever gave my mom was a grand-mother necklace. We never dreamed a woman could get so much mileage out of a simple gold chain with five little figurines.

Mom loved wearing the necklace. She said it was a way to keep the grandkids close to her heart. The thing was, you never knew how many grandkids were close to her heart. Some days all five might be on the chain; other days there might be only three or four.

"I see one of the grandkids is missing, Mom. What happened?"

"Your brother's youngest smarted off. I took him off the chain until he straightens out."

If one of the grandkids got cheeky, she took them off the necklace. She didn't really take them off, but she would fling their figurine around to the back of the chain. Swinging in style one minute, gone from glory the next.

She told whichever kids had been acting up that they could come back to the front of the necklace and join the others when they straightened out. She was a matriarch who knew how to hold a crowd.

Her antics with the grandma necklace were second only to the Great Pillow Caper. Mom and Dad, completely devoid of all rationality, once rented a huge van to take eleven of us a fair distance to a family reunion. It was a tight fit, elbows in one another's rib cages, window space at a premium, crying babies and cranky kids. Squabbles mounted on the long drive home. A dispute ensued between a couple of the kids over a pillow.

Grandma demanded the pillow be passed up front to her and announced she would "dispose" of the matter once and for all. She lowered her window. Then raised it. Then lowered it.

The kids were spellbound. Kids nothing — we all were.

Someone yelled, "Do it, Grandma! Show 'em what you're made of!"

Of course, she wouldn't really throw a pillow out of a vehicle window, which would be both illegal and hazardous, but it did keep the kids at rapt attention with the possibility that she might. The fighting stopped immediately. Those children, now all adults, are exceptionally well-behaved on long car trips but have an aversion to traveling with pillows.

Being that the grandma baton has been passed to the next generation, it only seemed fitting that I, too, have a means of holding a crowd. I now have a grandma necklace.

The grands know that I love wearing it and love keeping them close to my heart. They also know that jumping out of closets in order to hear me scream or commenting about my wrinkles will get them removed from the necklace.

Periodically, chaos erupts when we are all together and an instigator will run over, check the necklace to make sure he or she is still in place, then take off yelling, "I'm still on the necklace!"

"For now you are! Don't push it!"

THE BIG OUTDOORS

Six-year-old comes in from the backyard:
"I think I just saw a gardening snake."

Momma's Not Far From the Heart

She's tiny for 2 years old, on the petite side with delicate features and a voice like the whisper of a summer breeze.

She's tiny but tough. You have to be when you're the youngest of four.

Her mommy and daddy are gone today. They left while she was sleeping, just after midnight. They've gone to the hospital for the delivery of baby No. 5.

The family lives on the top floor of a Chicago Greystone more than 100 years old. The old house has huge windows with beautiful wood molding and ledges so wide an adult can comfortably sit on them.

She gingerly climbs over the radiator, which never gets more than a middling sort of warm, takes a seat on a window ledge and wraps her little arms around her little legs and pulls them close to her chin.

She's watching the action on the street below, cars passing, motorists parking, people walking briskly with morning coffee in one hand and cell phones in the other. Delivery trucks zip by and a mail carrier pushes a canvas-like wheelbarrow along the sidewalk.

She's OK with us here. She knows we're temps, fill-ins on duty for a day or two. She warms to us, but only to a point. Her heart of hearts belongs to Momma.

Her next-in-line brother has gotten out a microscope. He's peering at slides, alternating looking with his right eye, squinting with his left, looking with his left, squinting with his right.

Her next older brother is tinkering with squishy circuits, a conductive play dough in which he arranges electrical circuits and fires up tiny light bulbs.

Her big sister just brought up a load of a laundry from the cellar, three flights of rickety stairs down. Now she's doing a word search, working on earning a paleontologist badge from the National Parks Service.

Of course, it's not nearly as tranquil as it sounds. Skirmishes intermittently erupt and they all take turns testing Grandma and Grandpa's limits and reflexes. All except the little one.

Late afternoon, they are lined up on the sofa watching an animal show. From a distance it looks like the little one's eyes are glistening. Tears are welling.

I scoop her up and ask what's wrong. She looks in my eyes with a stiff upper lip and whispers, "Momma."

Tears tumble down her satin cheeks.

I hold her and soon she's fine.

After dinner, she climbs into the window again. Night has fallen and the length of the street is ablaze with headlights, taillights, stoplights and streetlights.

But it's not the dazzling lights holding her gaze. She's looking hard at each car, each passerby. She's looking for Momma.

When I pick her up to put her to bed, she rests her head on my shoulder, whispers "Momma," and starts to sob. Tears soak my neck.

I rock her awhile and sing a lullaby over and over. I lie

down next to her, my arm wrapped around her small body. The sobs slowly grow farther and farther apart, until they gradually come to an end. She finally falls asleep. I pull my arm away and wrap her big sister's arm around her.

She'll be at the window again in the morning, looking for the one who makes her feel completely safe and protected, the one who makes her eyes dance and her heart full.

Oh, that every child would know the warmth and strength of a loving momma.

Souvenirs

Because the husband is more a kid at heart than I am, he says we need to find souvenirs for the grands while we are on a trip to Savannah.

I can be a kid at heart, too, but I can also be a mathematician, and even cheap, tacky souvenirs times 11 grands adds up quickly.

The better half states that adults may be divided on the value of tacky souvenirs, but children are not. He says that children are of one mind on the subject — they like souvenirs and they want them.

So here we are at a tourist attraction, pawing through

mounds of cheap key fobs, plastic sun visors, kaleidoscopes, bubble wands, plastic alligators made in China, over-priced T-shirts and finding nothing. But then we spy the pirate section. On this we are in full agreement — you can never go wrong with pirates.

We consider a foam cutlass, but after a brief duel conclude that a foam cutlass creates more wind shear and sting than you might imagine. This would be enjoyed by the boys no doubt, but not appreciated by their parents. We opt for two pirate hats, which are soft and create no wind shear.

Still empty-handed for the nine girls, I spot small bracelets in an array of pretty colors all threaded on elastic.

"What about these?" I ask the husband.

He turns one over a couple of times and says, "Nice. But can you eat them?"

The bracelets are made of small beads shaped like fish and turtles, all resembling rock candy, which was popular when we were kids. We purchase nine and make a mental note to tell the girls not to try eating them.

As the clerk rings up the bracelets, I remember a souvenir I had as a girl. We had gone to the Gulf Coast and could choose one thing at a souvenir shop to remember our trip. I chose a blue plastic soap box with the lid smothered in silver glitter and topped with a pink flamingo and tiny seashells. It was cheap and tacky, and I believed it was the most exquisite thing a girl could own.

It was too beautiful to put soap in, so it sat in my top dresser drawer year after year, slowly aging, yellowing, the glitter falling off, but a reminder of a family trip long ago.

My dad once gave our girls unexpected souvenirs. They were in college at the time, far too old for trinkets. He hadn't taken a trip anywhere, but he had found small glass ornaments to hang in the window.

He has been gone more than ten years now. The girls are married and have families of their own, and those ornaments are still in their dresser drawers in their old bedrooms.

I have been won over to the notion that even cheap and tacky souvenirs may have worth and value. Tiny trinkets say, "I was thinking of you even though we were apart."

That message is always a good investment.

TUMMY ACHE

One of the little ones had terrible stomach pains, so her mother took her to the emergency room, suspecting her appendix.

After she had been thoroughly checked out, I asked how she was. "Fine!" she said, beaming. "And I still have my independence!"

What Dark Circles You Have, Grandma

You probably already know this, but in case you had any lingering doubts — if you are a grandma and someone wants to watch you put on your makeup, say no.

Bunking on the air mattress at our son's place in Chicago, I got up early, straightened my spine and staggered to the bathroom for my morning routine. After showering and dressing, I cracked open the door to let out some of the steam and was soon joined by a 6-year-old watching me put on my face.

"Why are you rubbing that stuff all over your face, Grandma?"

"Well, as you age your skin dries out and can look uneven. This helps fix it. You don't have dry skin. Your skin is beautiful just like it is."

"Oh."

"It can help wrinkles. You don't have wrinkles. Do you see mine?"

"Yes! On your forehead! One, two, three. And there's some on the side of your face, too! One, two — "

"OK, that's enough."

"My mom doesn't rub that on her face."

"That's because your mom is young and has beautiful skin."

"But my other grandma doesn't rub that on her face."

"That's because your other grandma has very good skin, too. She's the one who gave your mother good skin.

Now let's stop making this grandma feel bad."

"What are you doing with that pencil, Grandma?"

"Filling in some missing eyebrows."

"Where did they go?"

"I wish I knew."

"And now you're using the pencil on your eyelid?"

"Yep."

"What if you go outside the line?"

"Then it will be time to close the makeup bag."

"What is that, Grandma? Are you trying to straighten out your eyelashes?"

"No, it's mascara. It makes your eyelashes look thicker."

"Are your eyelashes missing, too?"

"Yes, they ran away with parts of my eyebrows. Didn't I hear your dad calling you?"

"No, he's still asleep."

"Too bad."

"What's that, Grandma?"

"It's concealer. It helps cover the dark circles under my eyes."

"How do you get those?"

"I got the concealer from the drugstore. The dark circles I got from raising children, being married to your grandpa and sleeping on the air mattress."

"Are you finished?"

"No. Every lady needs to put on one more thing before she's finished."

"What's that?"

"A smile."

AHOY!

I am putting on eyeliner, squinting in a mirror while three little grands watch.

"You look like a pirate," one squeals.

All three begin making "Aye, matey" faces in the mirror.

"You don't look like a pirate, Grandma," one says. "You look like a queen."

You Talkin' to Me?

The odds of having an uninterrupted phone conversation with your grown children, who are now parenting your beloved grandchildren, are roughly the same as you taking the gold in the next Olympics for pole vaulting.

I was talking to one of our daughters on the phone the other day when she abruptly asked, "Do you have to go potty?"

I was momentarily stunned. Perhaps she'd been watching some of those pharmaceutical commercials about problems that strike women of a certain age. I calmly said, "No, but thanks for asking."

When talking on the phone, it is difficult to tell when a question is directed to me or to someone else — say in the 2- to 5-year-old range.

"What are you doing out of bed? You're supposed to be asleep."

"If you thought I would be asleep, why did you call?"

Asking why I am out of bed is a close second to my all-time favorite: "Why are you crying?"

"I'm not crying. Why did you think I was crying? Should I be crying?"

Naturally, I understand our kids are often talking to their own kids, but I like to respond all the same, as it seems like more of a real conversation that way.

"We're out of dried fruit snacks."

"Thank goodness," I say. "Those awful things taste like

an old shoe."

Other times we can be in the midst of discussing a matter when I receive unsolicited instructions on how to dress.

"You'll need your coat and zip it up!"

"But I'm not going anywhere!"

The worst conversations are those in which the adult on the other end of the phone abruptly screams, "Noooooo! I have to go!" and hangs up.

You hope it's not a broken bone or involves a lot of bleeding. You don't exactly go on about business as usual because you're wondering if a little one is on the way to the ER. You'd call back but maybe the momma is still on the phone with 911. Maybe she's driving the kid to the hospital herself.

She finally calls back and says it was "nothing." Someone dumped one of those half-ton size bags of Veggie Straws on the floor. "Nothing" just took six months of my life.

It's not all bad. There are times I receive lovely compliments. "You look beautiful, Sweetie."

"Thank you. I've always looked good in black."

Sometimes the admonitions are invigorating. "Stop somersaulting off the back of the sofa and put those cushions back on right now!"

It's wonderful to think they still think I am capable.

I also love when we are attempting to make family plans and suddenly, with a great sense of urgency, one of them shrieks into my ear, "You didn't put that in your mouth, did you?"

"I did," I say. "It was an orange. There's nothing wrong with oranges, is there? Tell me they're not the new gluten."

Other times I don't take the interruptions so well and find myself getting defensive.

"Go get a tissue. You need a tissue."

"You go get a tissue!" I snap back.

Other times our fragmented conversations are quite agreeable.

"You eat that right now! Don't get up until you finish your plate."

"OK, if you insist."

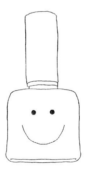

MANICURE

"Can you repaint my nails? I got so hungry in the night I ate the polish."

We're the Reason They Can't Go to Steak 'n Shake

One of the highlights of parenting is taking your children out to eat and having a stranger comment on how well behaved they are.

We know because it happened to us. Twice. OK, maybe it was only once.

As a realist, I am always sympathetic to the embarrassed mother with the wailing infant in her arms or screaming toddler plastered to her legs. Having been there and done that, I often smile and offer support by whispering, "Hang in there. Tomorrow will be better. Or worse. You never know."

Naturally, as grandparents, we wish for our grandchildren to be well behaved in public places and not create the sort of spectacles that wind up in online videos. When we took four of the grands to Steak 'n Shake, we went over the expectations for behavior. They all listened attentively and the 1-year-old responded, "Baa, baa, ack!"

Our server showed us to an isolated table at the back, near the restrooms. Perhaps she had a premonition. Every time she passed our table, she left another stack of napkins.

The kids were coloring, folding cardboard cutouts, patiently waiting for their food. When the server brought water (with lids), we placed them near the center of the table to avoid spills. Milkshakes arrived and they carefully put those, too, near the center of the table.

I nearly expected a stranger to stop by and compliment the children on their behavior.

A few moments later, the child to my right pointed out she had dribbled milkshake on her shirt. Reaching for napkins, I accidentally elbowed her milkshake and knocked it flat. Waves of strawberry milkshake flooded our side of the table, wave after wave rolling over the edge and cascading into my lap. I began catching milkshake by the handful, throwing it back into the glass, onto my plate and onto the table. The children were stunned. They'd never seen Grandma throw milkshake. The husband hurled napkins across the table. We frantically smeared milkshake from one side of the table to the other. My clothes were sticking to my body and my shoes were suctioned to puddles of milkshake on the floor.

Wordlessly, our server dropped off another round of napkins.

We hastened the eating along and the husband, being of the waste-not, want-not mind-set, offered a glass of milk still half full to the little one in the highchair. Never hesitant to express her displeasure, she batted the glass out of his hand, sending milk arcing like the St. Louis Gateway Arch, all of it showering the husband.

The server stopped by with more napkins. The kids cowered under the table and the baby wailed inconsolably.

As we stood to leave, the husband noticed that our pants were so soaked that we both looked incontinent. I considered that we might be stopped at the door and asked if we were responsible enough to manage small children.

We delivered the children back to their parents. Our own kids looked us up and down with our splattered shirts and wet pants, and chorused, "What happened to the two of you?"

"All you really need to know is that we tipped 50 percent of the bill," I said. "Oh, and don't be surprised if next time the kids don't want to go with us."

YOU'RE NOT AMISH?

Our 4-year-old grandson saw some boys in button-down shirts. "I just saw some Amish!"

Star Light, Star Bright

We have met the resistance. It is high energy, has sun-streaked hair from endless hours outside, considers Carhartt canvas overalls high fashion and even after a bath will still have dirt under his fingernails.

What is he resisting? What every child who has mourned the setting of the sun has resisted since the beginning of time — bedtime.

He has been out of bed for a trip to the potty, a drink of milk, a drink of water, followed by yet another trip to relieve his bladder and, several minutes later, an emergency trip to the bathroom because he forgot to brush his teeth.

He is back in bed now, but I can guarantee you he is not asleep.

Next on the agenda is the lighting phase of resistance.

"Grandma! It's too dark to sleep in here."

"No, it's too light to sleep at your place in the city. This is what night looks like. Dark."

I plug in a night light. I am nearly out the door, when a sweet voice whispers, "Can you turn on the hall light?

I turn on the hall light. I close the door halfway. I reopen the door. I readjust the door two more times to his precise specifications and return downstairs.

Five, four, three . . . "Grandma?"

"Yes?" Grandma says in a sweet voice, although it may not be entirely sincere.

"Grandma, I think I need a guardrail."

"You're in a double bed with a younger brother half your size, who I might add, has been asleep for an hour. Why would you need a guardrail?"

"He flops around. You don't know what it's like. He'll be all over me, arms, legs, punching, kicking. I'll have to roll to the side to get away from him and I'll fall out."

Grandpa puts in a side rail. We both head for the door, when a plaintive voice cries out, "You have ghosts!"

He is sitting up straight, eyes bulging.

"We do not have ghosts."

"Yes, you do. Listen."

"That's not a ghost. That is the neighbor's Airedale, Ollie, singing. It's kind of pretty once you get used to it."

"Does he know any other songs?"

"No, Ollie is a one-hit wonder. Now go to sleep."

Five minutes pass, six, seven . . . no footsteps, no running water, no toilet flushing.

"GRANDMA!"

"What now?" I call in a whispered yell, bounding up the stairs.

"The stars are falling!"

"This is the last time — " I walk in the bedroom and he's right. Stars are falling.

"I thought you'd like to see it."

"Of course, I would!"

They are glow-in-the-dark stars that our son put on the ceiling years ago. The adhesive has dried and they're falling, one here, a couple over there, like an indoor meteor shower in slow motion.

I sit on the side of the bed and together we watch the stars fall. We sit in silence watching the stars. His eyelids grow heavy and at last he is one with the night.

"What did it take?" the husband asks when I reappear.

"Nothing much, just a few falling stars."

The Big Muddy

The sky is blue, the sun is blazing and the aroma of SPF 60 sunscreen permeates the air.

The husband was up early wearing his bright orange hearing protectors, inflating the large pool that came in a box picturing clean-scrubbed, happy children at play. Inflated and filled, clear water in the pool shimmers in the dazzling rays of morning sun.

The whole crew is here today, 11 clean-scrubbed, happy grands just like the children on the box. Make that 11 plus one. A sweet 6-year-old neighbor boy from around the corner has joined the pack, making it a full dozen.

The kids are unleashed, running and jumping, splashing and screaming, younger ones taking time to wipe water from their eyes on fluffy clean towels.

Soon, two adorable little ones are using butterfly nets to strain bits of grass from the glistening pool water.

An hour later, it appears my colander is being used to strain even more grass and bits of thatch from the pool.

By 11 o'clock, the sun is nearly overhead, and the water is turning cloudy.

A 4-year-old whispers to her mother that she likes the neighbor boy. I considered sending the neighbor boy home.

By noon, the water is murky and the 4-year-old is giving the neighbor boy rides on the back of a tricycle as she circles the patio.

Grass and thatch cling to all their legs and arms but not a one of them cares. The children on the box would care.

The once clean towels are now soaked, matted and trampled. A 3-year-old runs by with a dried reed stuck to her back.

A 1-year-old, who only recently learned to walk, totters over with a water shooter in each hand. You have to wonder who she'll take aim at — her older cousins or the grandma who just cut off her supply of Cheerios.

After a lunch of PBJ and apples, the wild things dutifully line up for another application of sunscreen because it ain't over 'til it's over. The once beautiful lawn encircling the pool is an ever-widening mud slick. A tear glistens in the husband's eye.

By 2 o'clock, the pool water is a muddy brown. If kids who had not been here since morning came over and someone said, "Get in the pool," the kids would recoil in horror and run screaming.

By 3 o'clock the pool water appears to be morphing

from a liquid to a solid. The grandchildren are officially swamp people.

Cushions on the patio chairs bear mud prints and the beach towels are likely history. T-shirts and cover-ups that were once white are now the color of dirt.

At 5 o'clock, the neighbor boy's teenage sister arrives to pick him up. He paws through piles of flip flops and pool toys scattered throughout the yard searching for his tennis shoes and mud-colored T-shirt. On his way out the door, he politely asks my daughter, "Was this play or a party?"

"It was play," she says.

"Oh," he said, "I thought there might be a party bag."

"No, this was just play. You should see them when they party."

Get in Line to Hold the Baby

It's a shame that newborns can't talk. They probably have interesting observations on all the people constantly in their faces.

"That one needs to shave before he nuzzles my cheek one more time."

"Oh great, here comes that one with coffee breath!"

"I'd like to toss a couple of you in the air on a full stomach and see how you like it!"

The latest two babies in our family are probably asking what all the hollering is about. It's about everyone vying for a turn at holding a baby.

And you thought competition on the soccer field was fierce.

Three kids scramble to line up on the sofa, all wearing sweet smiles, all holding their arms in cradling position.

"I'm the oldest," one says, offering credentials.

"I haven't held the baby since this morning," says another, making a plea for pity.

The third one doesn't say a thing. She simply slides a pillow under her arm to demonstrate that she is safety conscious. Just like that, she gets the baby.

"I'm next! I'm next!" shout the other two.

I finally get a turn to hold the baby and a kid tugs on my skirt and says it's not my turn.

"I'm the Grandma," I say calmly. "It's always my turn."

She takes off crying that Grandma doesn't share.

If this high demand for holding babies continues, the babies will have to give up naps. Sorry, babies, it's just the way it is.

Another kid runs to one of the baby mommas and says, "Next time, you should have twins!"

I am holding the baby at the dinner table, the meal is finished, and five kids and four adults are on the other side of the table, all of them trying their best to make the baby smile.

They are bugging out their eyes, wiggling their eyebrows and uttering strange sounds. Frankly, none of them look very bright. One is shaking his head back and forth so hard that his cheeks are shaking. And he's the business exec in the family.

An array of fingers tickle her chin, her belly, the bottoms of her feet, all the while coaxing, "Come on, Sweetie, give us a little smile."

Then she does it.

She spits up.

Groans of disappointment.

We clean the baby up and they start in again, cameras poised, cooing, laughing, standing on their heads, hoping for a smile.

Grandpa finally gets a turn to hold the baby. He's had her 90 seconds when the baby's 2-year-old sister approaches, waves her hands in the air, wildly wiggling all ten fingers, saying, "I neeeeeeeed to hold the baby!"

But we all neeeeeeeed to hold the baby. Therein lies the problem — so many needy people, so few babies.

"I believe it's my turn to hold the baby," a voice says.

"Get in line," someone says.

"You just had a turn," someone else chimes in. "Why should you have another turn?"

"Because I'm the baby's MOTHER!"

She wins.

Sorry

As a grandparent, there's nothing you dread more than seeing one of your grandchildren in trouble. You'll gladly take the fall for them, which is exactly why we left the following note after a short stay with our daughter and her husband who have three little ones knee-high to a grasshopper.

Dear Daughter,

We had a lovely time. We would like to apologize for the condition of the bedroom you so graciously prepared for our visit.

We're very sorry about the sticky door handle. Please don't blame the twins just because they lathered their hands and arms with orange Popsicles. It was our fault. We often do that same thing at home and forget to wash. I can't tell you how many times we've enjoyed a good Popsicle melting in our hands and then left a trail of sticky orange on the walls, outlet fixtures, baseboards and door handles. We promise to be more careful next time.

On the subject of food, we're also sorry about the bits of crackers in the shag carpet. Ditto for the raisins and Cheerios scattered about. That was us as well who left the bits of graham crackers and Nilla wafers. You should know that we often bring food from home. Your father is afraid you'll put us on an all-lettuce diet and brings snacks in his suitcase. Yes, it is a coincidence that he brings exactly the same things your tots snack on, but any crumbs belong solely to us. We're sure your kiddos would never take food out of the kitchen (although you will find several of their snack cups under the bed).

About the bedding. You'll probably notice the dirty little footprints on the sheets and pillowcases. Those are our fault as well. We may have let the kids jump on the bed. We may even have held their hands so they could jump higher and told them it was a competitive sport. We know now that this was poor judgment on our part. Be assured that the next time we visit, we'll clean their feet first.

We feel terrible about the computer. We've never seen that particular diagnostic screen. Well, we may have seen it one time. It was after your little ones had been to our house. Just keep hitting the escape key and rebooting. It will all work out eventually. Don't worry if some of your financial records are missing. We hear the IRS is understanding about that kind of thing.

We hope the closet door went back on the track without too much effort. It's not like it was the first time someone had played hide and seek in there. As for that bent mini blind, it had no business being there in the first place.

We sure miss everyone, but there is something to be said for being back home where the carpet is crumb-free, the door handles are not sticky and we know exactly where to find the remote controls.

Love to the grandbabies,
Grandma and Grandpa

LIKE FATHER, LIKE DAUGHTER?

"I'm looking like Daddy.
My legs are hairy."

Flash Has a Party

We are still recovering from the birthday party of all birthday parties.

It was a child's birthday party. No pony rides, hired clowns or professional party planners. It was the birthday girl herself who put it over the top, the one turning 4 at a full gallop.

We thought it was going to be the usual: a few presents, some candles on a sloping cake accompanied by an off-key round of "Happy Birthday," followed by a sugar surge.

We were wrong.

The second we entered the house, her older sister whispered in my ear, "She's been in trouble ever since she woke up. It's been a rough morning."

When a 5-year-old says it's been a rough morning, you know it's been a rough morning.

A flash of purple shot through the room. Flash blasted up the stairs, down the stairs, rocketed out the front door, back in again, circled the family room, hurdled the baby in a single bound, somersaulted across the floor, yelling, "It's my happy birthday!" and blasted out the door again.

I regretted not having a lid for my coffee. And a padded suit.

In post-party analysis, the husband says it was to be expected. She'd witnessed a string of birthdays for others all summer long. At each and every one, she was front and center when it was time to blow out candles, her little face wedged beneath an armpit and a folded arm, radiating excitement.

Time after time, she watched as someone else opened the gifts, as someone else blew out the candles. She'd bottled it, suppressed it, contained it, then she woke up, knew she was 4 and simply exploded — like foam peanuts bursting out of a cardboard box and the grand finale of fireworks display on the Fourth of July. It was pure unadulterated joy, high octane exuberance.

They corralled her to open gifts and that's when it began — the falling unicorns. She loves those horse-like creatures with fluffy manes and a horn on top of their heads. She opened a unicorn beach towel, shrieked with delight and threw it toward the ceiling. She ripped open a large box containing a stuffed unicorn, squealed, and hurled it skyward as well. A unicorn nightgown was launched and then a unicorn headband.

"Heads up!" people yelled. "Incoming unicorns!"

Baby unicorns ricocheted off the ceiling.

"Somebody cut the ceiling fan!"

She bolted toward a straight back chair, climbed on top of it and began jumping up and down.

"Do you want to go to the ER on your birthday?" someone snapped.

Does the ER have unicorns?

She made a beeline to the table and stared at the candles on her unicorn cake. If intensity alone could have ignited them, they would have been shooting giant flames. It was the first time all day that she had been still. Poof! The candles were out and she was off, the joie de vie, joy of life, trailing her like a jet stream.

Apparently, Flash began sputtering around seven that evening and was out soon after. Her boundless exuberance was both entertaining and contagious. We may make throwing gifts in the air a family tradition.

Painting Like Georgia O'Keith

I was one of those mothers who believed that every moment was a potentially teachable moment. Not having learned my lesson the first time around, I continue exercising my somewhat misguided beliefs with our grands.

Since some of them enjoy painting, I thought we might do some intentional painting instead of just slinging paint on paper, the table and chairs and the walls like we usually do

We had art camp. It was more like art afternoon and camp was in the kitchen, but I was full boar intentional. I dug up a wonderful children's book on the American painter Georgia O'Keefe known for bright, bold close-ups of flowers, found jars to mix paint in and even scored some canvases on sale.

The small painters put on their paint shirts, or emergency clothes, as they call them. There is a wild assortment of emergency clothes in a drawer upstairs, which says a lot about what happens at Grandma's.

"I'm going to tell you about an artist named Georgia O'Keefe," I said.

"Did she live long ago?" one asked.

"Yes."

"Is she dead?"

"Yes."

The inspiration meter was flatline. I tried to rebound by showing them O'Keefe's paintings of eye-popping poppies, rich purple petunias and regal morning glories.

"What do you like about O'Keefe's paintings?"

"I like how O'Keith stayed in the lines."

"O'Keefe."

"Yeah, O'Keith."

"I like that she made the flowers BIG!" said another.

"I like that she didn't have a fit."

"Who said she had a fit?" "I think you've got that one upside down, Grandma," said the 4-year-old.

"No, I don't."

"Yes, you do."

It wasn't going the way I envisioned. Life rarely does.

I tinted jars of water with food coloring to show how to make different shades of colors. They tinted the jars of water with food coloring and turned them all a dark, muddy purplish brown — not a great color for painting flowers, but not bad for painting raccoons in the forest at night.

We talked about layering colors, painting something

larger than it is in real life and filling all the space on the canvas.

I explained that Georgia worked slowly, perfecting composition and layering colors for weeks and months at a time.

We filled a muffin tin with different colors of tempera paints, and they whipped out their paintings in 15 minutes.

One who announced she was painting a black-eyed Susan looked at her work, looked at an O'Keefe painting, looked back at her work and seemed satisfied. Then she dunked a big old, fat paintbrush in the blob of yellow and drew a great big sun in the corner of her painting. Then she put a happy face on it.

Another one said she was painting a zinnia. She looked at her work, looked at O'Keefe's and seemed pleased. Then she sat up straight and finished off her piece by painting her name so large it filled the bottom third of the canvas.

I think they were implying O'Keefe had room for improvement.

Don't we all?

ON TURNING 8

"Wow! I'm getting old really fast!"

On Writing

The older grands know that I am a columnist and have written several books. One of them even shared that bit of news in kindergarten. "I told them my grandma was a writer," she said, "but I didn't tell them about that book you wrote — you know, the one about you not being a very good mom."

She was referring to my first book, "I Was a Better Mother Before I Had Kids." Kids often have a skewed understanding of what the adults in their lives do. The grands do understand that I spend a lot of time at the computer writing.

One day, a couple of them wanted to know if they could help write a column.

"It's a lot harder than it looks," I said. I'm not positive, but I think they exchanged smirks.

They pointed out that they know their letters and can write both upper case and lower.

"You are qualified!" I said.

"What should we write about?"

"Well, you need a story to tell."

"Sometimes your stories are about us. We could write a story about you. How about we tell how you killed the bee?"

"Wasp," I said. "Accuracy is important."

"Yeah, the bee."

"Maybe," I said, "but you can't just say Grandma killed

a bee. You have to set it up, like a real story."

"I know," one said. "Write this — once on a hot sunny day."

"You've got the reader hooked," I said. "Then what?"

"Once on a hot sunny day I told Grandma I saw a very big bug flying in the birdhouse that's hanging on the play-house."

"Good, but you need to be descriptive. Paint a picture with words."

"We get to paint? Yeah! Let's paint!"

"No, you're writing a column. It's easy to get distracted writing, but a good columnist hammers out 25 words before getting distracted with something like painting or going to the 'fridge."

"OK. It was a very big bug and it had polka dots and it was flying and I said Grandma do you know much about bugs and then you said I know some and I said good because I don't know much."

"That's a run-on sentence."

"I wasn't running."

"Never mind. You can edit later. Or you can choose not to edit and give the editors something to do. Your story needs action."

"Grandma looked in the birdhouse and it wasn't a big bug — it was a bee. A bee with polka dots. Then Grandma took the birdhouse off the playhouse and put it in the yard. Then I said Grandma I still hear buzzing in the playhouse, so you came and looked and there were more big bees building a nest right on the playhouse. Did you type that the bees had polka dots?"

"That's not so much true," one says to the other.

"It is so. Didn't it have polka dots, Grandma?"

"They weren't exactly polka dots — but you could use your artistic license."

"Yeah, I want to use my lyin'-sense."

"A lot of writers do," I said. "Now end your story."

"Grandpa came with a can to spray the bees and Grandma said no that will make them mad and Grandpa sprayed them anyway and Grandma and Grandpa were yelling and bees were flying and Grandma killed some of them with a broom."

"We weren't yelling."

"You were yelling. That is true."

"You can't end a column with anger. That's what the rest of the news does. Leave the reader with a smile," I said.

"OK, write this: Knock, knock. Who's there? Boo. Boo who? You don't have to cry, it's just a joke!"

UNTITLTED

We've been watching some of the grands for a long weekend and it is Monday morning, which is my deadline for filing my column. One of them passes me at the computer and says,

"What are you doing?"

"I have to write a headline for a column."

"What's a headline?"

"It's like a title for a book."

"You mean like 'Little Red Riding Hood'?

"Yes, exactly."

"Why don't you call it 'The Three Bears?'"

A little later she sprints through the room and sees I am still working.

"The Princess and the Frog!" she yells.

Wunnerful

You can still catch Lawrence Welk on Saturday nights. Of course, that's assuming you want to. He's on PBS, still leading ladies across the dance floor, tapping the baton with "ah one, ah two, ah three," and cuing the bubble machine.

My three great aunts, who lived together in a two-story white clapboard house in Lincoln, Nebraska, used to watch "The Lawrence Welk" program religiously. It was like attending the United Church of Lawrence Welk with services every Saturday night at seven. The room was hushed, viewers sat quietly and watched with reverence.

Despite regular attendance, I lost interest in Lawrence Welk and we went our separate ways, although I doubt Mr. Welk noticed. Maverick that I was, I found myself more drawn to Ed Sullivan, who hosted acrobats spinning plates and a long-haired rock band from England.

Some years later, after I had married and became a mother, I heard a familiar "ah one, ah two, ah three" drifting into the kitchen one Saturday night.

Our preschool children were plastered to the television, transfixed by Lawrence Welk and his color-coordinated orchestra. They were mesmerized by the hairdos, hats and costumes, the sets, the singing and the dancing. At least the girls were. Our son wasn't that interested; he probably had something to dismantle somewhere.

"Back up from the television before those bubbles burst in your face, girls!" They did back up, all the way to the toy chest. They reappeared wearing play high heels, faux fur stoles and dress up clothes. They imitated the dancers on screen. They danced with each other and they danced with their dad, that night and many Saturday nights to follow.

Eventually they, too, grew older, lost interest in Lawrence Welk and his orchestra and Saturday night dances faded into history.

We hadn't heard from Lawrence Welk for some time. Then a couple of weeks ago when three of the grands were with us for the weekend, one of them asked if Lawrence Welk would be on television.

"Of course," we chimed, as though he was part of our weekend routine.

They stared with big eyes at puffy hair styles, bright costumes and a beautiful brunette singing her heart out in Spanish. They danced with each other and danced with Grandpa. The numbers that seemed dated to us were fresh to them. The warmth and affection of the performers appealed to the girls as much as the gowns and the gloves.

And then a baritone crooner sang, "Somebody Stole My Gal."

"What's a gal?" a small voice asked.

"It's like a girlfriend."

"Somebody stole his girlfriend?" another asked with concern.

"It sounds like it."

The three of them stood frozen in disbelief. There was palpable concern.

The next number began, and the camera zoomed in on

a woman playing trumpet.

"Is that a gal?" a small voice asked.

"Yep."

"Maybe she's the one he's looking for!"

Problem solved.

Cue the bubble machine.

Adios, au revoir, auf weidersehn.

THE BLACK EYE

Some grands were here while their parents were away for the weekend. Things got wild in the living room. A little one rolled off the sofa, knocked into the coffee table and banged her face.

"Looks like you're going to have a black eye," I said

"NO!" she yelled. "My eyes are BROWN!"

Once Upon a Time . . .

"Tell us a story about when you were our age," three of the grands clamor as we help put them to bed.

"Well, OK. When I was 6 years old, I walked 12 blocks to school every day."

"That's a long walk."

"It didn't seem long, although as I remember it was uphill both ways."

"Did any adults go with you?"

"No. Just other kids."

They gasp in horror.

"No, that was all right back then. Lots of kids walked to school."

Uphill both ways!" one adds.

"Exactly. And at the start of school a voice would come over the public address system and announce what would be served in the school cafeteria for lunch. Then the teacher would ask who would be buying lunch at school and who would be going home for lunch."

"Kids got to go home for lunch? No way!"

"Yes, way. You could go home for lunch if you didn't live far and could walk fast."

"But you lived far away, and it was uphill both ways."

"Yes, but I had three elderly great aunts who lived only six blocks from school. If I didn't like the school lunch, I raised my hand that I was going home for lunch."

"Who walked with you?"

"Nobody."

More looks of disapproval.

"Tell them that kids did that back then," I say to the husband.

He shakes his head as though he's never heard of such a thing.

"So, I would walk to my great aunts' house, knock on their door and announce I was there for lunch."

"Were they surprised?"

"I think so. They often let out little screams, which were probably squeals of delight. One would race to heat up chicken noodle soup; another would ask if I wanted crackers and a third would start cooking chocolate pudding. They'd sit me in a tall chair at the long dining room table and watch me eat. As soon as I finished, one of them would walk me to the end of the block and watch until I turned the corner to go back to school."

"That's a scary bedtime story, Grandma."

"It is not a scary story; it's a wonderful slice-of-life story. But one day my great aunts told my parents what I had been doing and that I shouldn't do it anymore, in case one day I came and they weren't home."

They shake their heads in agreement, siding with the voices of caution and disapproving of Grandma's actions as a 6-year-old.

I am quick to tell them they should never, ever do anything like that today, even though it was OK for me to do it a long time ago. Also, they should eat whatever the school is serving. Bedtime stories with grands should not end with strong caveats, but mine did.

They turn to Grandpa and say, "Tell us a story about when you were our age."

"Well," he says, stalling for time. "I always did what I was told and never disobeyed."

At least my story was true.

SOUNDS FISHY

After reading a bedtime story about how Jesus fed the 5,000 and had 12 baskets of leftovers, I asked, "What does the story teach us?"

"If you don't have food, eat leftovers!"

What Happens at Grandma's Stays at Grandma's

If I've told those grandkids once, I've told them 100 times, what happens at Grandma's stays at Grandma's.

I just received a frantic text from our daughter.

"The girls say you fed them ice cream for lunch!"

"And?"

"And nothing else. Just ice cream. Is that true?"

"Does that sound like us?"

"Mmmmmhmmmmm."

"Ice cream is in one of the major food groups. We got you covered for dairy today."

"Right, thanks."

"BTW, technically it wasn't lunch. We didn't feed them until almost 2, which made it more like an afternoon snack."

The week before that, we had kept a crew for a few hours and after they were picked up, we had another series of texts.

"I can't find the pants the baby wore to your house."

"What color were they?"

"Orange. The girls say you threw them in the trash."

"She had a blowout. The pants were beyond redemption. If you'd seen them, you would have agreed. You have better things to do with your time."

"OK."

"I'm sorry I threw them in the trash."

"That's fine. Don't worry about it."

"No, I mean the entire garage smells now. We should have burned them."

We're the ones watching the kids, but we're also being watched by them. They're stealth. They silently track our every move, make mental notes, then blab everything they see to their parents.

Overheard in the backyard:

"Grandpa got in trouble with Grandma while you were gone."

"What did he do?"

"He bought two more tricycles at the thrift store and then hid them from Grandma and pulled them out when we got here and Grandma says he doesn't need to keep buying tricycles, that four tricycles and three wagons are enough for us kids and the garage is full and a mess, but we like it when Grandpa keeps buying things."

"And then Grandma went back in the house and Grandpa said, 'Don't you kids worry, I'll keep buying fun things for you,' and then Grandma stuck her head back out the kitchen door and yelled, 'I heard that!'

"Yeah, we hope Grandma doesn't make Grandpa go to bed early tonight."

A phone call after an overnight:

"The kids say you let them watch a show with wolves with sharp teeth and they were chasing small animals."

"It was a nature video. I turned it off before the wolves started devouring their prey. Do you know the difference between a wolf and a coyote?"

"Why?"

"Ask the kids how to tell the difference between a wolf and a coyote."

Pause.

"They say a wolf is bigger, but a coyote has longer ears with sharper points."

"Then I guess they learned something, and you did, too. It was educational at Grandma's house."

It always is.

So, You Broke the Broom

She was sitting on a little wooden chair beside the piano, tapping her feet on the floor.

I finished my phone call and walked over to her, puzzled that her head was bent and she was looking down. It was an unusual posture for the kid who proclaims every single day of the year, no matter how dark the clouds, torrential the rain, searing the heat or bitter the cold, to be a "beautiful day!"

"What's up?" I asked, kneeling to look into her eyes.

"Well, I was outside — " she drew a breath and appeared to stifle a sob. "I was outside with the broom, sweeping by the garden."

Her chin trembled and her eyes began gushing tears as

she wailed, "I broke the broom!"

"Did you get hurt?"

"N-n-n-o-o-o," she sobbed.

"We don't care about a broom," I said, hugging her tight. "We care about you. There's not a single thing in this house we care about as much as we care about you."

More sobbing.

"Look at this old piano. See these scratches on the side? This piano has been around a long time. It's just wear and tear. Even if this entire piano somehow got broken, do you think we'd care about it more than we care about you kids?"

I realized it was ludicrous to use an example of a piano being destroyed. But then, considering several of her male cousins, maybe it wasn't ludicrous. Even if it were severely damaged during some bizarre boy antic gone awry, we'd still choose the kids over the stuff.

Her sobbing softened to whimpering, which was a step in the right direction.

"Come with me," I said, leading her by the hand. "Sit down in the middle of the sofa."

She sat down and a spring went BOING. She smiled a little half-smile.

"Now sit over there on the end. Hear that crack? That's the wooden frame! A lot of kids have played on this sofa, crawled over the back, rolled off the cushions." I didn't mention that I often stand on the end of it to reach books on the bookshelf.

"What do you think we care about more? The sofa or

kids?"

"Kids," she whispered.

"And look at that screen door."

Suddenly, I realized the house may be in worse shape than I thought. Oh well — such is the price of life and the joy of family.

"The only way the little ones can get that open is to push on the screen. We care about kids more than we care about the screen."

Finally convinced, she scampered back outside. A little later, I saw the "broken" broom on the patio and called to her.

"That broom was made to come apart," I said. "The handle and broom are separate pieces. You didn't break it— it just came apart!"

My lecture on the value of stuff as opposed to the value of people was probably unnecessary. But sometimes it never hurts to be reminded of what truly matters. It makes for a beautiful day.

K - A - T - E

One of the grands runs into the kitchen and breathlessly asks, "Grandpa, how do you spell Kate?"

She is clutching an index card and marker. Clearly, it is a matter of great urgency. The kids are playing school and making a name tag for the youngest.

"I'm not sure I understood you," he says.

His ears aren't what they used to be, and to complicate matters, the girls have high-pitched voices that sound like squeaky little mice.

How do you spell Kate?" she asks again.

"Cake?"

"No, KATE!"

Still not comprehending, he says, "Use the word in a sentence."

"Ok," she says. "How do you spell Kate?"

He Said, She Said, They Said

How is it that a group of people can be in the same house at the same time, experience the same event, yet have markedly different memories?

The way I remember it: Five grandkids were here for a long weekend and it was loud. Very loud.

The way the kids remember it: Five of us cousins were together for a couple of days at Grandma's. We used our inside voices.

Grandpa: A couple of the grandkids spent the night. Maybe two nights. Or three. If it was loud, I didn't notice.

Grandma: The kids spent one morning crafting at the kitchen table. There was construction paper everywhere, scissors all over the place, markers without lids, glue sticks rolling on the floor, tape that wouldn't peel off the roll, a jammed stapler and a hole punch that had opened from the bottom and showered the floor with confetti. One kid had marker on her face, and another had marker covering both sides of both hands. The tablecloth we use when they craft was a smidge on the table and mostly on the floor.

The kids: We made art. Wanna see it?

Grandpa: It may have gotten a little wild at the kitchen table. I didn't really notice. The tape was old and kept getting stuck. I was focused on unsticking the tape.

Grandma: It was time for lunch, so I said, "Clear the table, then go wash your hands."

The kids: Grandma said go wash your hands, so we did.

Grandpa: I helped with lunch by keeping the kids out of the kitchen. I moved the coffee table out of the way in the family room so they could do cartwheels and somersaults.

Grandma: I cleaned up the crafting mess, boiled water for mac and cheese, made a few sandwiches for the peanut butter-only wing, peeled and cut apples, halved some bananas, cooked the macaroni, set the table, threw in another load of laundry, finished the mac and cheese, iced a head bump that mysteriously happened in the family room, put the milk on and called them to the table.

The kids: Grandma is a good cook and we told her so.

Grandpa: I walked into the kitchen and there was lunch. It's like magic.

Grandma: After lunch, I said, "Why don't you kids clear the table and dry a few dishes?" They each grabbed a dish towel and pulled up chairs next to the kitchen counter. I washed, they dried. I finished washing before they finished drying and went into the other room to pick up some toys. I folded laundry, straightened up the bathroom where they had washed up and cleared a path in the front hall.

The kids: After lunch Grandma went into the other room. We think she sat in a chair. The sink was filled with dirty dishes. We cleaned up the whole kitchen all by ourselves while Grandma sat in a chair.

Grandpa: She looks well rested to me. Those kids are a huge help every time they come.

Pretty as a Picture

I have just been handed a new portrait of myself. I look like someone who got off the Space Mountain ride at Disneyland and needs medical attention. Or like someone who staggered out of a bar at 3 A.M. after a night of binge drinking. Or like SpongeBob SquarePants' grandmother — SpongeBob's deranged and demented grandmother.

It's not bad, considering it came from a 3-year-old. She meant well. At least I think she meant well.

I have new appreciation for the personal secretary of Clementine Churchill, who set fire to a portrait of Winston, which was commissioned by the British Parliament on his 80th birthday and was loathed by both the Churchills.

Does one torch a portrait done by a grandchild?

No, not one this funny.

My eyes are askew, and I have a crooked smile, overlapping eyebrows and curly hair wherein each curl looks like a tiny contorted worm. The whole package is encased in a square body, hence the SquarePants family resemblance.

Maybe I'm being vain, but I didn't think I was the shape of a square. At least not yet. Maybe I'm delusional. They say we never see ourselves the way others do.

Do we ever like pictures of ourselves?

Personally, I prefer all close-ups of myself to be taken at a distance of at least 50 feet.

We often think we look better than we do. Then, when we see candids of ourselves, we are sometimes taken aback.

Me? That's me?

Who did you think it was?

The camera doesn't lie.

Thankfully, Photoshop can.

I will say the SpongeBob SquarePants Grandma drawing is better than a portrait another grandchild did. At only age seven, the child went for stark realism, drawing in every wrinkle and laugh line. My face looks like an unforgiving all-cotton sheet left in the dryer too long.

I've given the kid 30 days to redeem herself.

In the child's defense, I come from a family of wrinkles. Both sides. My mother, whom I will always love for her dark sense of humor, used to comment on my nice skin, then cup her wrinkled face in her hands and say, "Behold your future."

The publicity photo I use is several years old and should probably be updated with a more current one. A new publicity photo isn't as simple as it sounds. There's an art to the publicity photo. You want it to look nice, but not too nice. If it is too nice, people won't recognize you when they meet you in person and will feel tricked and betrayed.

It is far better, albeit mildly humiliating, to send out a realistic photo and have people pleasantly surprised when they meet you in person.

"Your photograph doesn't do you justice."

Mission accomplished. Wince and say, "Thank you."

I may start sending out my SpongeBob Grandma portrait. People should be thrilled when they meet me in person and ask how long my recovery took.

DOUGHNUT DASH

We are making a doughnut run with some of the grands in tow. The husband is reading the coffee choices off the menu board. "Caribou Roast Coffee"

"Dream Beam Coffee"

"Jamaican Me Crazy"

"HEY! THAT'S WHAT MY MOM SAYS EVERY DAY!"

Drive-by Fruiting

I was the victim of a drive-by fruiting last weekend. I was buzzing about in the kitchen, vaguely aware of a small shadowy figure on the other side of the door leading to the garage. Frankly, there are a number of shadowy figures when 22 are here for a meal, so I didn't think much about it.

Then I heard BAM! BAM! BAM! I looked at the door to see cherry tomatoes exploding, sending juice and seeds sliding down the glass. Sliding, sliding, sliding. The tomatoes looked remarkably similar to the cherry tomatoes dropping from the half-dead vines in the raised bed in the backyard.

And to think some grandmas hold grandchildren on their laps and read them stories.

My sister-in-law, married to my brother and the mother of two boys, clucked her tongue and quietly cleaned up the mess. She knew that at a different time, in a different place, it could have been any of hers doing the drive-by fruiting.

I was reasonably sure I knew who the offender was. OK, I knew beyond a shadow of a doubt. I raised the kid's father. They have the same DNA.

We got lunch on the table and everyone was seated and eating when I calmly announced there had been a crime wave in our neighborhood recently. The perp briefly looked up from his PBJ with big eyes, then immediately looked back down.

"We ourselves were a victim of crime this very day," I said. "I was working in the kitchen, preparing lunch for all of you, when I heard BAM! BAM! BAM! at the kitchen door."

The perp continued nibbling his sandwich, avoiding eye contact. All the other kids were transfixed with eyes as big as saucers. Some nuts are harder to crack than others.

"I turned to see what it was and saw cherry tomatoes splattered on the door to the garage. Can you imagine how shocked I was? I was stunned!"

He's not buying it. He's knows it takes a lot more than a hit with three cherry tomatoes to shake this grandma.

"I thought about reporting the crime, calling the police. Then, just as I was ready to dial 911, I had second thoughts. What if the person who did this did it on an impulse, without thinking? What if the person who did this was sorry for what he did? (I was narrowing the field with the male pronoun; he still didn't budge.)

"I've done some things I regret. And I've had some second chances along the way. Maybe the person who pelted my door with tomatoes needs a second chance. Maybe he's sorry right now and wants to say so."

No, he did not want to say anything.

"I believe in second chances," I said. "Does anyone else around this table believe in second chances?"

His hand was the first to shoot into the air.

Later that afternoon he was outside and one of his uncles lifted him up to see in the kitchen window. A line of cherry tomatoes sat ripening on the windowsill.

You bet I did. Two of them. You should have seen him jump. The knowing grin on his face said it all: "She's smarter than she looks."

A Beetle in the Freezer

There is a beetle in my freezer and he's not there by accident. I caught him, I boxed him and then I froze him.

If you're an insect lover, you may want to stop reading now. But before you leave, know this — there's no better way for a bug to go. Millions of them go like that every fall with the first hard freeze. Initially, I felt a bit remorseful about freezing a bug, but then I realized I was merely hastening nature's cycle.

I only hope the beetle saw it the same way.

In any case, the beetle is in the freezer on top of a pack of ground beef and between two bags of frozen vegetables. Now, if I peel the lid off that box in two weeks and find the beetle is missing, I will probably throw out the ground beef, the vegetables and everything else in the freezer.

It is my son and grandson's fault that there is a beetle in the freezer. Frankly, I often gag slightly when I hear about their latest exploits. Then, before I know it, I am taken in by the excitement and doing things I never envisioned doing — like catching insects and casually popping them in the freezer.

They recently bought a casting resin kit (liquid plastic that solidifies in an hour). A lot of crafters use the kits for making jewelry or preserving leaves. Our son and his son are using the kit to preserve insects in test tubes. I suppose their bug casts could double as jewelry, but I don't think they will become a fashion trend anytime soon.

So far, they have cast a lightning bug, a carpenter ant and have a dragonfly chilling. (Because they have nature projects in their freezer far more frequently than we do, we often order out when we pay them a visit.)

Shortly after they told me about the project, I spotted a shiny black beetle crawling on some brick. Every fiber of my being wanted to crush the beetle, whack it with my shoe, flatten it with a rock (I've been very pent up lately), anything but catch it. But when I considered what a little boy can learn studying the wonders of creation up close, I was suddenly on board.

Apparently, I was so on board that when I called to let them know that I had a specimen in my freezer, suddenly, unexpectedly, with no forethought whatsoever, I heard myself commit to scoring an earwig.

Who am I? I cannot even say the word earwig without screaming. *Earwig* (noun): bug that slithers into your ears while you sleep and spin wigs. Maybe not, but if not, why do they call them earwigs? They're disgusting. And now I'd committed to finding one.

Just like that, I'm an entomologist. Or an etymologist. Or both.

Unbelievable. Of course, there's always the chance I won't come across an earwig under a mound of mulch or in the seed pods on the false indigo where they hang out every year. But if I do, I am honor bound to try and catch it.

Gag.

Make Mine a Double

A friend was in the restroom after my mother's funeral, when a woman washing her hands at the sink next to her said, "I know it's wrong to be jealous, but I was always jealous of Virginia. She loved her family so much and was so close to her grandchildren."

The woman was right. My mother loved with exuberance. The flip side of loving much is hurting much. That may be especially true of grandmas.

We were all devastated when my brother's oldest son was diagnosed with a disease that would steal his sight. The entire family was in shock, stumbling in a fog of disbelief. I remember sitting on the sofa, sobbing, begging God to make it not so.

My brother and his wife didn't have the luxury of sitting and sobbing. There were doctor appointments, tests, more tests and a 13-year-old son to prepare for the onset of darkness.

Life drags you forward by a ring in your nose even when you don't want to go.

The anguish was all encompassing. Mom's was unrelenting.

"I wish I could take my eyes out and give them to him. I don't need them anymore. I wish I could give them to him."

She said it time after time, phone call after phone call. "If only I could. If only I could."

She meant it. If she thought it would have worked, she would have done it herself right there at the kitchen table.

She was a grandma who loved with a fierce love and now grieved with a sorrow of equal intensity.

One day an older friend, who was already a grandma, said to me, "Your mother hurts twice. She's a grandmother hurting for her grandson, and she's a mother hurting for her son and his wife."

It was a two-generation heartache.

Mom became her grandson's greatest cheerleader. It wasn't always a pat-on-the-back, softly whispered words of encouragement type of cheerleading. Her style was more direct. Sometimes it bordered on confrontational. She dished the medicine she thought you needed.

She encouraged my brother and sister-in-law any way she could. One day she took my sister-in-law shopping for a new bedroom suite because the bedroom furniture they had was old, hand-me-down and too small for their needs. She thought my sister-in-law could use a pick-me-up.

Go big or go home. That was Grandma.

If a mother's favorite child is the one who hurts the most, so a grandmother's favorite grandchild is the one who hurts the most.

Mom could not take her heart off her grandson. Not when the tests showed he'd lost more peripheral vision, not when tests showed the few degrees of central vision remaining were like looking through a window screen, and not when a reprobate on the school bus sucker punched him in the side of the face and said, "Bet you didn't see that one comin', did you blind boy?"

What the reprobate didn't know was that my nephew's little brother was on that school bus, too. He's the "little brother" in age only, not size. He is a football player by size. When the reprobate got off the bus, little brother was waiting. He punched the kid and said, "That's for my brother."

Of course, both boys lost bus privileges, but in hindsight the thing that stands out is how fortunate that reprobate was that Grandma wasn't on the bus.

Mom cheered on her grandson at every bend in the road just like she cheered on my brother and sister-in-law. Then she died too young after a brain aneurysm and missed the best part — the part where life opened up and her grandson hit his stride.

The first step was partnering with Casey, a beautiful German Shepherd leader dog. Casey gave my nephew new mobility, independence and confidence.

With Casey, my nephew did a little college, worked a couple of jobs that were so-so and then found his place. He landed a job assembling outdoor faucets, the kind you attach a garden hose to on the outside of the house. As a boy, my nephew had always watched and worked alongside my brother who is a talented jack-of-all-trades.

Off my nephew and Casey go to work each day in a warehouse. He holds his own alongside sighted workers, and has received accolades for his output.

Grandma would have been over the moon. She would have been phoning everyone in her address book, shooting out emails, pinning down strangers in the grocery store, telling them about her grandson and his accomplishments, because that's what grandmas do. They love double, hurt double and brag double.

The Family Tree

Explaining you were a mommy before you were a grandma to a young grandchild quickly becomes a who's who of considerable complexity.

"Grandma, Mommy said that you were her mommy."

"Yes, and I still am," I say. "I could ask her to unload the dishwasher right now and she'd probably do it."

"Really?" the child exclaims.

"Yes. Before I was a grandma, I was a mommy, and your mommy was my little girl and now my little girl is grown up and is your mommy."

This is the strangest thing the kid has ever heard. Naturally, I try to help by putting it in context.

"Your mommy was a little girl and I was her mommy a long time ago before you were born."

Turns out, this is a horrible follow-up. There is no more disturbing statement for young children than to hear there was a time when they didn't exist.

What do you mean before I was born? How can that be? When was I not born? Where was I? What an awful, terrible time that must have been!

In an attempt to clarify, I muddle things even more. "Yes, I was your mommy's mommy and Grandpa was her daddy."

This is too much. Not only is the child to believe that Grandma was once a mommy, but that Grandpa was once a daddy. Hey, the kid has eyes and she's thinking there's no way the two of them were ever that young!

The child gives me the once over and slowly says, "So you were a mommy . . . Grandpa was a daddy . . . and Mommy was one of your kids?"

"Exactly!" I shout.

Silence. The wheels are turning.

"Then, before you were a mom . . . were you a kid, too?"

"Yes!"

Wisely, I keep my mouth closed about being a kid so long ago it is what we now call the "last century." There's only so much backward time travel small children can comprehend.

"So, Grandma, when you were a kid, did you have other kids in your family?"

"Yes. John was my brother."

"You mean Big John?"

"Yes, Big John was my little brother."

"How could he be your little brother when he's bigger than you and we call him Big John?"

"He wasn't always bigger. As a matter of fact, I am three years older and for a long time I was bigger than he was and

I would boss — oh, it doesn't matter what Grandma used to do to her little brother, because he grew way bigger and he's still making me pay for teasing him years ago. The main thing is to be kind to your brothers and sisters no matter who is older or younger or bigger or smaller."

Satisfied, smiling and with a twinkle in her eye, she dashes off to the front room where her cousins are playing and shouts, "Guess what? Grandma used to be a kid!"

The Mermaid Challenge

Holidays do strange things to grandparents. Take Halloween — it made me think I can sew.

I was driving one of the grands home and she was rattling off what everyone was going to be for Halloween. She said she really, really, really wanted to be a mermaid this year, but she couldn't.

"I don't have a costume and Mom said we're not spending money on Halloween costumes."

"You could make one," I said, slowly inching toward a giant sticky trap for humans.

"I saw a picture of one, but you have to use a glue gun to make it. I'm a kid, Grandma. I'm not allowed to use a glue gun."

I glanced in the rearview mirror. Her eyes drooped, her mouth drooped, even her little shoulders drooped. She was

122

resigned to the fact that she would not be a mermaid.

"I could probably make one out of things you buy at JoAnn's," she said wistfully, "like that JoAnn's we're driving by right now."

She didn't ask, she was just dreaming. I began dreaming with her. Actually, it was more like an out-of-body experience, because I heard my voice say, "Maybe I could make you a mermaid costume."

Did I mention I haven't sewn in a decade? That, even when I did sew, most of my projects turned into square pillows?

"Really?" she squealed. Her cheeks flushed with roses, her eyes danced and her smile sparkled. She was ecstatic, like she'd just won the Publisher's Clearing House Sweepstakes.

"You'll probably have to find out how to make one," she said, bubbling with excitement. "When do you think that would be? Want me to call you tomorrow to find out? What time should I call?"

The kid had visions of a glittering Disney mermaid costume and I was wondering if Duct Tape comes in green.

"I'll think about it tonight and call you tomorrow afternoon," I said.

My phone rang the next day at two minutes past noon. It was Excitement calling.

"Is it done yet?"

Not quite. I'd found something on Pinterest that looked doable — doable for someone with patience and talent, both of which I have little.

Like I let that stop me.

That night I battled a monstrosity of pink netting that kept growing and growing, filling the entire kitchen. As I rethreaded the sewing needle for the thirteenth time, neighbors may have heard screeching pierce through the windows. That would have been me asking an empty room why the mermaid's mother didn't just buy her a costume!

If a little girl comes to your door trick-or-treating and looks like she's wearing a giant green tube sock with an uneven pink ruffle at the bottom, it's one of our grands.

For the love of children, pretend you think she looks like a mermaid.

I told her not to let anyone examine her costume up close because I don't want others taking my good ideas. I also said she should walk fast, but take tiny steps.

The costume isn't great, but it may do the trick.

The Nearly True Story of the First Thanksgiving

There's a lot of grumbling that young people don't know history like they should. If we're honest, we must acknowledge an inherent problem to being young and learning history. The younger you are, the more there is to learn.

Curious, I asked five members of the youngest generation in our family (preschool through early elementary) for the story of the first Thanksgiving.

What follows is "The Nearly True Story of the First Thanksgiving."

"The king said they weren't allowed to worship God so the Pilgrims wanted to come to America where they could do what they wanted. They picked a ship called the Mayberry."

"No, I think they came on the Mayflower."

"It was a long trip. It took a year, maybe two. The kids played games on the ship, mostly soccer, but also some tic-tac-toe."

"There was a captain on the ship and he had guiders who helped guide the ship."

"The Pilgrim ladies wore blue dresses. They looked like Mary and Laura from Little House. The men wore blue shirts and jeans. Pilgrims were like pioneers."

"Some of the people on the ship got sick and died. A baby was born on the ship. His name was Oceanus."

"They sailed and sailed until someone said they saw land."

"They landed at the Mayflower. There was a rock that said Mayflower right where they were landing."

"They didn't have much food and were very hungry."

"They ate fish and probably berries out of the woods. The men went out to hunt deer and bears. I don't think I would eat bear meat, unless I was super hungry. I bet I would if I was super hungry."

"More Pilgrims died that winter. Maybe more than half. We think they had little pox. In one family, both the mom and dad died and one girl had to live alone. She only had herself."

"Only two families survived without losing any family members. One of them was Oceanus' family. None of the people in his family died."

"In the spring, a couple of guys were hunting for food and they saw an Indian. He helped them learn how to plant and harvest and where the lakes were and how to weed and other good stuff and how to make fire."

"And he helped them bury the fish in the ground."

"When fall came, they wanted to celebrate and called it the First Thanksgiving. They were going to celebrate that they were alive, so they had a big feast."

"They had turkey and deer, potatoes and carrots, ham and chicken."

"The Indians brought popcorn. Salted popcorn. The Pilgrims had never seen that before."

"They played a lot of games. The moms might have knitted mats for checkers and cut wood from trees like checkers. Oh, and they might have carved chess sets, too."

"Did you get the part about popcorn? Salted popcorn."

"They played and ate and thanked God for letting the Indians be nice to them and they thanked that one special Indian for helping them learn their way."

And there you have it — a composite account of the first Thanksgiving as told by the historians of tomorrow.

SUBSTITUTE TEACHER

When we kept a couple of the grands for a few days, their mother told them that Grandma was going to be busy, but Grandpa would help them with their school work. One of the kids looked Grandpa up and down, then said, "How do we know he knows anything?"

Thinking Inside the Box

One of the delicate balancing acts that accompany grand-parenting is gift giving. First, there is the question of how much. How much is enough? How much is too much? Does the grandparents' giving overshadow the parents' giving?

There is also the question of whether to give a gift that is fun or a gift that is educational.

Go for fun and you score big with the children, thereby elevating your status in the highly competitive world of grandparenting. Do you want to be the grandparent remembered as the one who gave socks, or the grandparent remembered as the one who gave the drum set?

Go for educational and you score big with the tots' parents, who give an approving look that says, "Thanks for not rotting our children's brains."

The truth is, we know from experience what the most wonderful gift is for the younger set. We've seen it happen a hundred times.

Someone helps a little one open a gift. The thoughtfully chosen wrapping paper is tossed aside, the gift is studied and handled for a few moments, and then it is tossed aside, too. The little one then reaches for the gift that delights the senses, thrills the imagination and elicits chortles, chuckles and belly laughs — the empty box the gift came in.

Last year we gave one of the little girls a large doll that came in a large cardboard box with a cellophane window. The real hit was when her preschool brother crawled into the box, positioned himself in the cellophane window, and his older brother dragged him from room to room asking what people would pay.

Yes, it's the empty box that is the big hit. Could someone please turn off that annoying educational toy?

Look at her, wearing that box like a hat. She has made herself disappear and is giggling. What could be funnier than disappearing on a major family holiday (a question I often ask myself).

The hat grows passé and the box becomes a storage tub as the little one throws everything within reach into it.

The storage tub is emptied and the tot climbs into the box, now a means of transport. Siblings and cousins shove the box around the house, careening around corners, sliding across hardwoods and clipping door frames.

Meanwhile, a small educational ride toy that lights up, plays music, recites the alphabet and teaches how to count in two languages sits forlorn and forsaken in a corner.

The tot now has her favorite blanket and is nesting in the box for a moment of calm. She casts us a wistful gaze that says, "When will you grown-ups ever learn?"

O CHRISTMAS SHE,
O CHRISTMAS SHE

"If a Christmas tree has a skirt, does that
mean it's a girl?"

Home Alone

I read the email to one of our daughters over the phone and heard my voice crack.

"Where does he live?" she asked. "Is he close by?"

"I have no idea."

The email was responding to a lighthearted column I'd written wondering if the grands would still come around when they've outgrown the inflatable pool and can't be lured with Oreos. The column triggered a flood of responses, many relaying the joys of older grands who still greet them with big hugs and even bigger smiles.

And then there was his email:

Dear Lori,

I will soon be 96 in a few weeks. I am a widower with grandchildren in their 40s. My great-grandchildren range from 12 to 17. Two thirds of them live within a few minutes from me. The rest are a few hundred miles away.

Granted, they are all busy people, doing meaningful things. They are happy and healthy and for that I am very grateful.

As the years go by, the distance between us gets wider.

I am not looking for, or asking for, anything. I am not seeking accolades from anyone. But it would be nice, as well as comforting, in my older age to know that they care or even think of me. I guess the word I am trying to say is respect. Is that asking too much?

I rarely see or even hear from them. I make excuses to myself, but it grieves me. They, especially the great-grandchildren, are growing up and I am not in the loop. That is sad! Very sad!

At this stage of my life, what else is there to look forward to?

I guess just knowing they are well, happy, and safe, will have to suffice. But, does it?

Taking Flight

I'm not sure how much longer the two of us can fit into this wicker chair together, but for now we fit just fine. Snug, but fine. She's a willowy thing, long legs, hair flying in her face, serious one minute, pure goofball the next. We are on the porch leafing through the Sibley Backyard Birding cards.

"Did you know a swift can sleep when it flies?" she says.

"Is that right?" I ask. "How do you know that?"

"We read it in a book."

"Amazing," I say.

"Yep, amazing," she echoes.

Amazing is that she looked a whole lot like a baby bird herself when she was born, just over three pounds. Now here she is sitting strong and healthy, neurons firing, feet swinging, talking about birds, bicycles without training wheels and cartwheels.

"Amazing," I say. It really is.

"Look at this one, Grandma. We've seen this one."

"Looks like that blue jay slicked his hair back with mousse, doesn't it?"

She giggles, leafing through the bird cards lickety-split. The stack is in disarray and cards are tumbling in every direction. This is exactly how she's growing — with amazing speed, with life and learning cascading in every direction.

"Listen," she whispers. "A woodpecker. Do you hear?"

Oh, I hear. I heard when she cried nearly nonstop the first six months of life, when she babbled first words and now as she chatters nonstop about her new shoes, trips to the library and how she's stuffy from allergies.

A robin swoops over to the crab apple tree and perches on a branch.

"Look up his song, Grandma."

I play the robin's song on my phone. "Cheer-up, cheer-up, cheerily." The robin in the tree answers, singing, "Cheer-up, cheer-up, cheer-up."

"He's talking to your phone!" she squeals.

"Phone call for Mr. Robin on line one, please."

She is beyond delighted and I am delighted that she is delighted, knowing that these moments will pass us both by all too quickly.

The robin swoops down to the lawn. She watches him intently, wondering what he might find and speculating that he probably has a nest nearby. The robin hops around, pecks a couple of times and pulls out a fat, juicy worm. He tilts his head as if to show us his catch. And then he takes off.

"Look at him fly," she says.

I'm looking. Believe me, I'm looking.

Always Room for More

We are on Round 61, or thereabouts, of the Rotating Stuff game where family members try to get rid of their stuff by leaving it with other family members to put with their stuff.

We first began playing the game when the kids went to college. They always came home with far more stuff than they left with. When they went back to college each year, they left a lot of the extra stuff behind in bedroom closets, on shelves and under the bed.

"Mind if I leave a few things here?"

"Sure," we said, "There's always room for more."

Sometimes I stood in the doorway of their rooms and shed a tear thinking, "They're gone but at least we have their stuff."

We let their stuff be. We let it gather dust and watched

as it silently multiplied into more stuff.

Whenever one of them graduated, got a new job and moved into a new apartment, we immediately seized the opportunity to take all their old stuff and move it in with their new stuff.

"How have you managed without these two large wooden oars, snowshoes and 17 crates of art supplies?" we asked.

The score was back in our favor. But not for long. When they each got engaged, they moved back home for a few months before their weddings.

"Mind if I bring some of my stuff?"

"Sure," we said. "There's always room for more."

They brought more stuff. Bigger stuff, heavier stuff. Furniture, small appliances, a beat-up pickup truck with dual exhaust. The neighbors loved it. Especially when our son fired it up at six in the morning or came home late at night.

The day after they each walked down the aisle and said, "I do," we quickly began moving their stuff out of our place into their place.

The key to winning the Rotating Stuff game is generosity. When you give their stuff back, give 10 times as much stuff as they gave to you.

They started having babies and we started accumulating more stuff — cribs, Pack 'n Plays, high chairs, potty chairs, sound machines, baby monitors, blankets and toys.

Pacifiers and diapers filled what were once empty dresser drawers. Sippy cups, plastic dishes, bibs and child-size forks and spoons were crammed into the pantry.

"We're running out of room," I muttered.

"The closets are beyond full," the husband lamented.

Then the youngest called. Her little family has out-grown their small home and will be moving. Could we help store some of their stuff?

"The garage is full," the husband said.

"The attic is packed," I said.

"What do you need space for?" we asked.

"Three little girls, my husband and me."

It will be five months before they can get into their house, a new build.

Sure," we said. "There's always room for more."

This 'Fridge Ain't Big Enough for the Two of Us

We knew the closets would be full. We knew there would be toys and baby gear covering the floors. We even knew the garage would bulge. What we didn't know was that the most densely packed space in the entire house would be the refrigerator.

Our local newspaper once ran a feature titled, "What's in your 'fridge?" in which they published a short paragraph listing what people had in their refrigerators.

Make a list of what is now in our 'fridge and you're looking at a 300-page book. And that's just Volume No. 1.

Want balsamic vinegar? We have it in triplicate. Ditto for soy sauce, mustard and ketchup.

Pickles? You could open a deli. Cheese? Cheddar, Swiss, Parmesan, Asiago or mozzarella? Would you like that in blocks, slices or shreds?

The problem isn't that the contents of two refrigerators merged into one, but that two women can't stop shopping. Two women, neither of whom can, nor ever will, yield control of the kitchen. The kitchen is where dynasties are built. Nobody yields a dynasty.

There was an initial agreement to meal plan together and shop once a week. It lasted until I was able to find my keys, swing by the store and pick up a few things.

Then she slipped out of the house, stopped by the store and picked up a few things. There is so much slipping in and out and swinging by the store that some days we nearly crash our cars in the driveway.

Turns out, our agreement was an agreement made in mutual bad faith.

Do you know what happens when two women try to rule the same kitchen and keep stopping by the store to pick up a few things?

There is an explosion — an explosion of leftovers.

We now have 29,765 small containers stacked in the 'fridge with a few bites of this and a few bites of that. We live in fear of the day they all go bad at the same time, emit fumes, blow their sealed lids and blow up the refrigerator.

The explosion will probably take the entire kitchen with it. When the dust clears and the last of the pasta finishes sliding down the walls, we will both still be standing, still battling for control.

Our daughter keeps explaining that we can avert disaster if I will simply abide by her meal-planning chart that shows the menu for each night and the ingredients needed for each meal.

"When you write the ingredients down with the meal you are making, you will always have what you need," she calmly explains.

I nod as though such a concept is entirely new to me and note that the meal schedule says we are having cilantro honey-lime chicken tonight.

"Did you get cilantro?" I ask.

She gasps.

"I'll get my car keys."

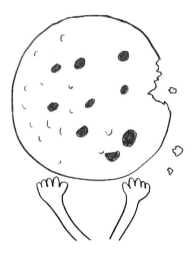

GIVE A KID A COOKIE

To a kid who asked for a second cookie: "You already have one cookie you're eating. Why do you need another?"

"I want to be ready for when this one is gone."

Me and My Shadows

Since our daughter, her husband and their three little ones moved in with us while waiting to move into the house they're having built, I've had a most peculiar feeling.

It's an odd feeling, as though I am not entirely alone.

Oh, I catch glimpses of shadows now and then, long hair flying around a corner, muffled laughter, but I often do not see to whom the shadows, the hair and the laughter belong.

They're quick, very quick.

I dash up the stairs and the faint echoes of footsteps trail behind.

I stop, the echo stops. I resume the stairs, the echo resumes.

Sometimes I feel as though there is a presence behind me and other times it feels as though a presence has gone before me.

I turn into the bathroom to put on my makeup and see my cosmetic drawer is ajar. I would never leave it like that. Or did I? Or did someone else? But who? It's unlikely the husband has developed an interest in blush and mascara. The hairbrush and comb are out of place. Two of my lip glosses have lip gloss sliding down their sides and are without caps.

I straighten the drawer, fix my face and step into the bedroom.

Indentations have pockmarked the bed — like divots

on a golf course. Odd. The bed was made more than an hour ago. Muffled giggling comes from the other side of the bed and the bed appears to shake ever so slightly.

Strange, simply strange.

I return downstairs and pause at my desk. The tape dispenser is empty. Again. For the third time in three days. I don't remember using vast amounts of tape. Maybe I need more sleep. Maybe I tape things in my sleep.

The stapler is open and empty as well. Surely, I would remember flying through 100 staples. But then I don't remember creating this pile of drawings with colored markers — pictures of people with beady eyes, crooked smiles, wild hair and stick bodies with disjointed arms and legs.

The scissors are out as well. They're the good scissors, the pair that is sharp and not for children. Strange, I don't remember cutting. Something among the pieces of paper lying on the floor catches my eye. It is a long golden curl of hair. I don't remember cutting my hair. What's more, I don't remember being blonde.

I mutter aloud, "When did I use up the tape? When did I empty the stapler? When did I create these wonderful, beautiful drawings?"

The door to the closet beneath the stairs softly closes. Laughter emanates from behind the door.

Creeping to the closet ever so silently, I fling open the door and yell, "GOTCHA!"

The phantoms tumble out, roll on the floor, arms and legs flying in every direction, screaming and shrieking with laughter.

"You scared us! How did you know we were in there?"
"Oh, just a lucky guess."

Oh Baby, What a Workout

People often ask how it is going with a preschooler, a toddler and an infant living with us.

The truth is, we have settled into a lovely and comfortable routine, brought about, in part, by our willingness to live amid an obstacle course.

The various baby contraptions, small furniture pieces and assorted paraphernalia scattered throughout the house have become more or less permanent fixtures. As such, they have rerouted traffic patterns and altered many of our basic movements. Our reflexes are sharper than ever, we burn more calories each day and are closing in on long-standing fitness goals.

Before their arrival, we simply walked from one room to the other with no cardio or stretch benefit whatsoever. Now the doorway from the kitchen to the dining room is occupied by a Jolly Jumper, a bulky contraption on a spring, suspended from the overhead door molding. The baby sits in the jumper seat and bounces up and down screaming with glee. To get from the kitchen to the dining room, we give the contraption a gentle hip bump, elongate our entire bodies, inhale deeply to minimize our girth, stretch until we can stretch no more, then slither through the small opening between the contraption and the door frame.

Our flexibility has improved dramatically, and we are both five inches taller.

A portable bassinet in the family is parked in front of the access area to the bookshelves. If you want books, a brief run and short hurdle over the bassinet will get you there. Reading, once a passive activity, now leaves us breathless.

The baby walker is less negotiable, as it has big feet and is easy to trip over. When the baby walker appears in your path, it is best to turn sharply, cut a wide swath around it, then resume speed.

Further benefitting our cardio, we often take the stairs two at a time. A baby crying, preschoolers wailing, glass breaking or the sound of water rushing from unknown origins and we are on our way!

It feels good to be running track again.

The Bumbo, a molded plastic seat the baby can sit in, has been a challenge, as it is frequently mobile. It may be in the kitchen one minute, behind my desk chair another, or under the piano bench. You never know if it will be occupied by baby or by a life-size baby doll that scares the wits out of you. The Bumbo has been hard on our blood pressure, but we are adapting.

Even the downstairs restroom is a challenge. To wash your hands, an adult must lean in at a precarious angle over a step stool used by the girls to reach the sink. The hand towel will be on the floor or halfway in the sink, but never on the towel bar. We disdain predictability.

We've never been more fit. Who knows what we'll do when they leave. Probably just sit around, grow sedentary and out of shape.

And cry our eyes out.

Return to Order

They're gone now. Those dirty rotten kids.

Just like that, they up and left and took three precious little girls with them.

Their new house is finally ready. What was supposed to be a five-month stay with us turned into six and six turned into seven. The builder's timeline was train-wrecked by snow, cold and rain. What else is new? Their closing date was moved back three different times and three different times I thought our daughter was going to crash and burn. Anticipation delayed is crushing. But then it happened. It really, really happened. They signed the closing papers and fled.

They moved out while we were out of town for the weekend. Our daughter warned us the house looked like a wreck. Only the upstairs, really. It looked like a rental property, where the renters fled in a frenzy because the sheriff was on the way to serve an eviction notice.

Dresser drawers askew, disheveled bedding, closets sheltering empty hangers, random clothes and shoes. Storage boxes jutted out from beneath the beds.

They were eager to go, and who could blame them? It had been close quarters.

Shared kitchen
shared meals
shared family room
shared driveway
shared privacy
shared head colds
shared stomach bug
shared influenza

Four of us got influenza. We fell one after another just like dominoes.

At least the baby was spared. But maybe she had built additional immunity from the room where she was sleeping. It had once been our son's bedroom, but the husband claimed it when he retired. Proclaiming himself the family historian, he has filled the room with towers of books, old newspapers and magazines, genealogy records, printouts of census records, old photographs (some mural size), hand-drawn enormous family trees, notes and emails from family historians, old letters, old diaries and a vast assortment of quirky memorabilia. From dust to dust to Ancestry.com. He comes from a long line of "collectors."

The room can emit a near visible cloud at times. We

cleaned it best we could before setting up the Pack 'n Play for the baby in the near center of the room. There was no considering the Feng Shui or aesthetics of the arrangement; it was the only open space. It would be, what's the word? Cozy?

The setup seemed to agree with the baby. She nestled in, falling fast asleep at naptime and bedtime to the pulsing heartbeat of her sleep machine. Then she began waking up from time to time around midnight or 1 A.M., which was odd, because she'd been on such a good sleep schedule when they arrived.

One night, as our daughter staggered semi-conscious toward the crying across the hall at 1 A.M. she glimpsed the husband trotting down the stairs with a pile of family records in his arms.

Busted.

He confessed that he sometimes slipped in for papers he needed. He was sorry. But sorry didn't mean it was the last time he crept in to raid his archives.

The room is still full of papers, journals and family records, but without the Pack 'n Play, it echoes a vacant house kind of emptiness.

The newfound quiet is exactly like we thought it would be. Deafening.

I'm lost without my morning alarm.

I often got up early when they were here, around 4 or 5 A.M. to log a couple of hours working before the rest of the house awoke. It was a trick getting downstairs, knowing just where to step on creaky hardwoods. Bare feet or socks.

Shoes made more noise. I always creaked somewhere. If not the floorboards in the hall or on the top two stairs, it would be my left knee popping.

I'd make my way to the kitchen, flip on the light, wait for the coffee to brew and savor the splendid peace of a full house at rest. Then I'd settle in at the computer keyboard, start working and soon be suspended in a time warp — until I was jolted by the sound of boulders crashing through the ceiling overhead. I'd jump in my chair. I knew what the thundering was, but it never failed to startle me. Nothing more than a 3-year-old and 4-year-old sliding out of bed at 7, tumbling onto the hardwoods, eager to greet the day.

They'd traipse downstairs hand-in-hand, still sleepy-eyed, and softly say, "Good morning, Grandma."

"Good morning, Sweet Things."

If I got the edge on them, I hid behind the sofa. They knew where I was, but I'd jump out anyway, and they'd act surprised and scream and I'd act surprised and scream.

Mornings are quieter now.

Less defined. Less exciting. Less screaming.

They've been gone several weeks, and we are still separating the tangled threads of theirs and ours. Our foldable baby rocker or theirs? The baby walker was ours, right? Small bike helmets in the garage? Theirs. Big black duffle bag with neatly organized power tools? The son-in-law's.

He is a master craftsman, that one. Can do anything, fix anything, build anything and does not shy from a challenge. Fortunately for him, we offered many. He repaired our screen door, installed new fixtures in the master bath shower, switched out the rickety dead bolt lock and door knob on the front door for a new one, replaced the belt on the washing machine so the entire kitchen doesn't shake like an earthquake in progress when the machine is on spin cycle, fixed the drain in the tub and installed a new instant hot water dispenser under the kitchen sink.

Just for fun, or out of boredom, one cold and dreary Sunday afternoon he took apart the cuckoo clock that hasn't worked in 30 years.

"Have you ever worked on a clock before?"

"No."

"Think you can fix it?"

"We'll see."

He was at it for hours. Meticulously, tediously tuning and fine-tuning until all the mechanisms were in sync. It works.

Cuckoo. Cuckoo. Cuckoo.

I am, in part, now cuckoo at times — nearly gleeful to have some space back, with ample room and quiet in which to work and to not have the day pierced with intermittent crying. At the same time, it is a palpable ache to have some space back, ample room and quiet in which to work, to not have the day pierced with intermittent crying.

It wasn't always easy, but it was good. So good.

I found the girls' sweet library bags the other day, the ones their momma made. They were tucked in a basket behind the wingback chair. They'll need those soon. They go to the library every week.

She brought her sewing machine with her when they came, often setting it up in the dining room after the girls were in bed, along with the ironing board, a cutting mat and large storage tub crammed with fabric. She made baby blankets for friends with newborns, car blankets for her own little ones and personalized pillowcases from fun fabrics for the nieces and nephews at Christmas.

I miss the purr of the sewing machine at night.

The house is slowly returning to the look and sound and feel of empty nesters. The indoor play tent has been put away. The love seat cushions remain on the love seats. You can walk across the kitchen floor without the crunch of Cheerios underfoot. The plastic tablecloth has been stashed on a shelf in the hall closet. Washable markers, crayons and safety scissors are once again organized in boxes in the craft cupboard. And the tape. Oh, how they love tape. I just peeled another two pieces off kitchen chairs.

I swing open the doors to the pantry cabinet and a whole lot of empty stares back at me. No more big bags of Veggie Straws and Goldfish. No more pouches of applesauce or juice drinks in boxes. The 'fridge looks bare as well. The industrial-size tubs of yogurt are gone, as well as our son-in-law's favorite condiments — Tabasco, sriracha, horseradish, pickled jalapenos — basically anything that sets your gut on fire.

We won't be eating as much mac and cheese as we did when they were here. Ditto for flour tortillas. We'll be back to food for the aging based on a diet of fear — fear of heart attacks, fear of stroke, fear of high cholesterol. Skinless chicken, fish, salads and vegetables are once again the norm.

I'll miss them. The carbs that is, not just the kids.

The little ones wove themselves into every hour of every day. They jumped in the leaves Grandpa raked in the fall and sat on the front porch watching the rain fall in early spring. Grandpa often carried them two at a time on his back for horsey rides. He's a soft touch and they knew it. They'd sweetly ask him to build a fire in the fireplace and the man would race for firewood. Then they'd sweetly ask me for hot chocolate. OK, so maybe I also raced to fill their every wish and desire, too. Why not? The pleasure was all ours.

We were spoiling ourselves, not them.

The basket with baby wipes and diapers still sits on the dryer. That little baby has the fattest cankles in the entire world. They actually crease. She spent the better part of the first year of her life here. She'll probably be walking by the time we see her next. It was a gift to hold her in our arms before she could escape.

I found one of her most treasured pacifiers today. I'm looking at it, wondering if I should or I shouldn't.

What kind of Grandma holds a pacifier as ransom until she can see the kids?

REMEMBER WHEN

The girls were back for the first time since the big move. They went from room to room, mesmerized by how differently things look now that they no longer live here and every square inch isn't packed with boxes and storage tubs. The 3-year-old looked around the family room, now void of baby blankets, toys, puzzles and books, and whispered to no one in particular, "I used to live here when I was young."